Overcoming Dyslexia

Overcoming Dyslexia

Resource Book 1

By Hilary Broomfield

W

WHURR PUBLISHERS
LONDON AND PHILADELPHIA

First Published 2004
Whurr Publishers Ltd
19b Compton Terrace, London N1 2UN, England and
325 Chestnut Street, Philadelphia PA19106, USA

British Library Cataloguing in Publication Data

A catalogue record for this book is available from the
British Library.

ISBN 1 86156 398 1

Printed and bound in the UK by Hobbs the Printers,
Southampton, UK.

Contents

Introduction

This teaching programme is based on the highly successful handbook *Overcoming Dyslexia Second Edition* by Hilary Broomfield and Margaret Combley (Whurr 2003). The materials can be used on their own or in conjunction with the handbook and can be used as part of the literacy hour or specialised support lessons.

The activities are suitable for learners of all ages who are developing their basic literacy skills. The approach taken is a multi-sensory one, which aims to lead the learner from the development of early concepts about print, phonological awareness and the alphabet through to the confident use of letter sound links for reading and spelling words and sentences. There are also sections on working with two-syllable words, simple suffixing, and learning irregular words and common homophones. Those familiar with the *Overcoming Dyslexia* handbook will recognise these from part one of its 'step-by-step' approach. A second resource book for part two is planned.

The materials include background information for the teacher, teaching and learning activities, guidance notes for parents and homework activities. There are also separate sections on assessment and planning. The programme is suitable for use by learning support assistants under the guidance of the teacher and is compatible with the requirements of the National Literacy Strategy at Reception to Year 1 and the beginning of Year 2.

Although the resources include a wide range of literacy activities, they should always be used as part of a more extensive literacy programme that includes reading for enjoyment, experiencing a variety of text types and further opportunities to develop literacy skills through real life situations.

All the resources are photocopiable. For ease of reference a set of symbols are used to organise and identify activities. These are explained on the following page.

Symbols

 Information and background reading for the teacher

 Teacher-led activity
Activities with this logo will need a teacher or assistant to lead them and explain what is to be done.

 Pupil Activity
This work may be carried out individually as independent work or as guided work in small groups.

 Advice for parents and carers
The parent information sheets provide background on literacy topics which may be useful when carrying out homework activities and supporting literacy at home.

 Homework
Activities with this logo can be given to pupils as homework but may also be used as follow-up activities in class for small groups or individuals.

 Assessment and Planning
Assessment materials for each area of literacy are included in the end section along with advice on planning learning objectives and lessons.

Concepts About Print

The phrase 'Concepts about Print' (CAP) refers to a learner's understanding of how books and printed languages work (see Clay 1993). That is to say, do they understand the directionality of books and print, how letters are organised into words, words into sentences and sentences into texts? Do they know how punctuation marks are used and how they should be responded to? The assessment on page 156 will help you check these.

Even quite sophisticated learners can have some gaps in CAP knowledge. The author once tried to teach paragraphing to an advanced learner, but had to backtrack to work on 'sentence' when it became obvious that the learner misunderstood 'sentence' for 'line of text'.

To ensure that concepts about print are understood clearly, we need to check that we are all using the language of literacy in the same way. For example, many children (and some adults!) interchange the use of 'letter' and 'sound' which causes confusion in the classroom. Some children mistakenly think that 'letter' means a capital letter and that 'sound' means a lower case letter.

Activity Sheets

The CAP symbols on page 4 provide extra visual clues to learners who are having difficulty remembering what is expected of them when they are asked for the name of a letter or to say a sound. It can be used in conjunction with the memory cards described on page 58.

The Punctuation Marks on page 5 can be used as a memory aid for pupils when they are writing or as part of a punctuation game during shared reading when pupils hold up the appropriate mark at the right point in a story or supply missing punctuation marks that have been edited out of a text.

The Beginning Middle and End activities on page 6 are for learners who have not yet grasped the meaning of words such as 'first', 'last', 'middle', 'beginning', 'end', 'next', 'before', and 'after' who will struggle with literacy work in the classroom. Without this understanding how will they know what to do when they are asked to 'Look at the last word in the sentence' or to tell the teacher 'Which letter comes after 'j' in the alphabet?'

Integrated reading activities

These 'Concepts About Print' (CAP) activities can be built into your everyday teaching sessions, particularly shared reading. Make a note on your lesson planner which CAP skills or terms you want to address and build them into the lesson organisation.

Make sure they are fun and don't take the reader's enjoyment away from the book.

- Look at the **title** of a book. **How many words** are in the title? Which is the **first word** of the title? The **last word**?

- Find the **author's name** before beginning to read. What is the **first letter** of the author's **first name**? What is the first letter of the **surname**? Where is that **letter** in the alphabet? How would that help you in a book shop or library?

- Scan for **words** on a page **beginning** or **ending** with the **letters** or **sounds** you have been working on.

- Scan a text that has been read for **words** that have **one letter, two letters, three letters**, etc. Which is the **longest/shortest word** you have read today?

- How many words with **capital letters** can you find? When have capitals been used to begin a new sentence? When do they show that the word is someone's name or the name of a place? Have capitals been used for any other reason?

- How many **full stops** are there on a page? What do you notice about the next letter after a full stop?

- How many **question marks** are there on a page? What are the **answers** to the questions?

- Were there any **exclamation marks** in your reading today? How did you read those bits of the story?

- Find a piece of dialogue within **speech marks** and write it on **speech bubbles**.

- Choose a **sentence** that has been read, write it out and cut it up into individual words. How many **words** are there in the sentence?

- Photocopy and enlarge a short section of text. Can the learner cut the text into separate **sentences**? Which is the **longest/shortest** sentence?

See also the homework activities on page 8–10

3

Symbols

Name the letter.

Say and listen to the sound.

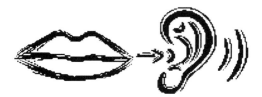

Point to the picture.

Read the word.

Punctuation marks

Capital letters

ABCDEF

<u>A</u> capital letter is used at the beginning of a sentence. <u>T</u>hey are used for the first letter of a name like <u>P</u>at or <u>I</u>pswich

Full stop

A full stop is used at the end of a sentence when it is a statement<u>.</u>

Question mark

Do you always put a question mark at the end of a sentence when it asks a question <u>?</u>

Exclamation mark

Hey there<u>!</u> Don't forget to use an exclamation mark at the end of a sentence when it is written with feeling<u>!</u>

Speech marks

Put speech marks at each side of the words people say. <u>"</u>Like this,<u>"</u> said Hilary.

Speech bubble

Speech bubbles are used in comic strips. The words that people say are inside.

Beginning, middle and end

The following step-by-step sequence is a useful guide to ensuring learners understand the concepts of 'beginning', 'middle' and 'end' in preparation for sequencing sounds within spoken words. The beginning, middle and end sequencing board on page 66 can be used alongside these activities as a visual and physical support.

Many will not need such a detailed approach at all, but some will. Some will move through the steps very quickly, perhaps covering several in one lesson. Other learners will need to work at a much slower pace, whatever is right for them. When they are ready to work with sounds within words, move on to the activities with phonemes on page 30.

Learners who need to work at this level will also find the wealth of activities in *Sound Linkage* (Hatcher 2001) extremely useful.

Working with real Objects

1. Place a set of 3 objects/pictures in a line, for example, three toy cars – ask the pupil to point to the car at the beginning of the queue, the one in the middle, the car at the end, etc. Mix up the required responses and the items.

2. Link the previous activity to the beginning, middle and end (BME) sequencing board on page 66. The pupil should place the objects/pictures at the beginning/ middle /end of the board. Mix the required response and items.

Using Familiar Names

3. Tell the pupil a list of three names, e.g. Paul, Carl Sam. Ask them which name is at the end/beginning/middle of the list? Do not use written names, this is a listening activity.
4. Now link the previous activity to the BME sequencing board. After listening to the sequence of names without being able to see them, the pupil should select matching name cards and place them in the same sequence at the beginning/ middle/end of the board. Repeat this with different sequences of names. Photographs can be used if the pupil is unable to read the names.
5. Say a list of three names e.g., Robert, Tom, Carl. Ask the pupil the question 'Was Carl at the beginning, middle or end?'

Concepts about print

Working with Colours

6. Say a list of three colour words e.g., blue, red, and yellow. Ask the pupil which one is in the beginning/middle/end. After hearing the sequence, the pupil should put coloured counters in the same sequence on the BME board. Repeat with different colour sequences.
7. Say a list of three colour words, blue, red, yellow. Ask the question 'Was red at the beginning, middle or end?' Repeat with different colour sequences.

Using Percussion

8. Play a sequence of 3 percussion sounds behind a screen, e.g. bell, shaker, drum – then show the instruments and ask the pupil to identify which sound was at the beginning/middle/end.
9. After hearing the sequence the pupil should place pictures of the instruments in the right order on the BME sequencing board.

Moving on to Letter sounds

10. Say a list of 3 random letter sounds, e.g. c-t-p. Pupil says which sound was at the beginning/middle/end.
11. Repeat the previous step working only with sounds that the pupil can match letter shapes to. After hearing the list of sounds, the pupil should be shown the three corresponding plastic letters and how these are placed on the BME sequencing board. Now repeat this several times using the same letters but in different sequences. Each time after hearing the full list of sounds, the pupil should put the plastic letters on the BME sequencing board and say the sounds in correct sequence. Note that at this point the difference between vowels and consonants has not yet been introduced. Once learners move on to working with real words (see page 30) they should use the consonant, vowel, consonant board (CVC) on page 66.
12. Say a list of 3 random letter sounds, e.g. c-t-p. Ask if 't' was at the beginning/middle/end?

Literacy homework

Name

Return by

Finding Capital Letters: What to do

You will need the front page of a newspaper.

1. How many capital letters can you find on the page?

2. Underline them with a felt tip pen.

3. What do you notice about when capital letters are used?

This work had: **Parent signature/comment**

☐ no help

☐ some help

☐ a lot of help

Literacy homework

Name

Return by

Words and Letters: What to do

You will need a magazine, comic or newspaper.

1. Find six different words you can read.

2. Cut out the words and stick them on a piece of paper.

3. Count the number of letters in each word.

4. Write the number of letters next to each word.

5. Which word is the longest and which is the shortest?

This work had: **Parent signature/comment**

☐ no help

☐ some help

☐ a lot of help

Literacy homework

Name

Return by

Listening to Sounds: What to do

Say these words to your child. They should not be able to see the words. Ask them to say if the sound / / is at the beginning of the word or at the end.

_____   _____   _____   _____

_____   _____   _____   _____

_____   _____   _____   _____

This work had: **Parent signature/comment**

☐ no help

☐ some help

☐ a lot of help

Phonological Awareness

Phonological awareness is the ability to focus on the spoken sounds that make up our language. It is a listening and speaking activity that maps onto written language through letter sounds. Difficulty with phonological awareness frequently correlates with problems in literacy. Training in this area is felt to have significant impact on progress if it is closely linked to making the connection between sounds and their corresponding letters. Key to this is the awareness and manipulation of syllables, rhyme, alliteration, onset and rime and, most importantly of all, the sequence of individual phonemes within words.

Understanding the Terminology

Syllables are the 'beats' within words, which give our language rhythm. The word 'cat' has one syllable; the word cat-er-pill-ar has four.

Rhyme is when we focus on the endings of words to hear if they sound the same, as in 'cat' and 'hat' or 'write' and 'sight'. Note that it is the sound of the words that is the same, not necessarily the letter pattern. Our regional pronunciation of words will affect whether they rhyme or not.

Alliteration is when words begin with the same sound such as 'slippery slope' or 'Gentlemen Jim'. Again note that it is the **sound** that is the same not the letter.

Onset and Rime refers to the natural units of sound within syllables. An onset is the initial consonant or consonants at the beginning of a syllable, e.g. the /c/ in 'cat' or the /sl/ in 'sleep'. The rime is the vowel and everything else that follows within that syllable; e.g. the /at/ in 'cat' and the /eep/ in 'sleep'.

Words of more than one syllable have more than one onset and rime. 'Magnet' has two syllables, /mag/ and /net/. Each of these can be broken into its own onset and rime, e.g. /m/ (onset) /ag/ (rime) and then /n/ (onset) and /et/ (rime).

Syllables which begin with a vowel sound have no onset, just a rime. The word 'insect' has two syllables, /in/ and /sect/. These are divided into the rime /in/, the onset /s/ and the rime /ect/.

Phonemes are the individual sounds in our speech. The word 'sit' has three phonemes /s/ /i/ /t/. The word 'ship' also has three, /sh/ /i/ /p/ even though it has four letters. The sound /sh/ is one phoneme represented by two letters. Some phonemes are represented by several letters, such as the sound /i/ when it is represented by /igh/ in the word 'sight'.

Leading Activities

Listening First – Carry out the activities in this section as listening games first. This makes sure the learners are focusing on the sounds **they hear** and not the letter shapes they see. The words and letter sounds being discussed should only be visible to the teacher. Once you are sure that attention is on the sound pattern then a link with the corresponding letters and words can be made.

Initially, some learners find this focus on sounds difficult and tend to use their visual memory for letters and words instead. Watch out for the pupil who always gives a letter name when asked for a sound or gives the word 'chips' or 'circle' when asked for a word beginning with the same sound as 'cat'. Pupils such as these, who rely heavily on visual strategies, may benefit from some work with **non-words** that follow regular sound patterns to ensure that auditory skills are also being built into their repertoire. Examples of these are 'zim', 'prum', 'staz', 'chule'.

The Skills – Each area of phonological awareness practised here involves two different skills, sound **blending** and **segmentation**. We use **blending** skills when we try to read an unfamiliar word. First we identify the individual letter sounds and then we blend them together to **build up** the whole word. **Segmentation** is used when spelling an unfamiliar word. Here we start with the whole word and then **break it down** into its sound sequence before writing it down.

Vocabulary – Make sure the learner understands and differentiates between the terms **sound** and **letter**. Try to be consistent in your own use of these terms to avoid confusion. Use **letter** and **letter name** to refer to letter shapes that can be seen or written. Letter names never change. Use **sound** to refer to the phonemes that we hear. There are over 40 of these and the way in which they are represented by letters does change. One phoneme may be represented by a range of different letter combinations, for example /ā/ can be written as 'a' 'ay' 'ai' or 'eigh'.

You also need to be sure the learner understands concepts such as **first, last, beginning, end, middle, next to, before** and **after** and can apply this to listening work. If not this is where you need to begin (see page 6).

Saying the sounds – When working with letter sounds try and pronounce them as **purely** as possible and to encourage your pupils to do the same. Try not to use an exaggerated 'uh' or 'er' sound on the end. This can result in difficulties when trying to blend the sounds together, with c-a-t becoming 'cuh-a-ter' !

Counting Syllables

I went shopping and I bought.......

 1   2   3

Have pictures of food items or empty food packages as additional support. Attach numbers to carrier bags representing the number of syllables in the food words. Pupils should identify which carrier bag the food item should go into according to the number of syllables in the word. There are some suggested items below.

1 syllable – eggs, bread, milk, fish, rice, crisps

2 syllables – apples, cornflakes, sugar, peanuts, carrots

3 syllables – bananas, sausages, spaghetti, marmalade, chapattis, margarine

'Top of the Pops'

Make Compact Disc shapes from shiny card or use the reverse side of unwanted free CDs and number these to represent the number of syllables in words.

Ask pupils to list ten performers that they like and create their own top ten.

They should then identify how many syllables are in each performer's name and link these to the right CD,

e.g. Oasis (3 syllables), Atomic Kitten (5 syllables)

See also the homework activities on page 16–19

Blending and Segmenting Syllables

Syllable Smoothies

Blend together the syllables in the names of fruits to create a smoothie! Make sure you leave a one second interval between each syllable. The children should repeat the syllables as you have said them and then blend them together.

Can you and the children come up with any more?

Ap-ple	black-ber-ry
o-range	co-co-nut
ki-wi	pine-ap-ple
le-mon	sat-su-ma
me-lon	ba-na-na
man-go	marsh-mal-low
va-nil-la	tan-ge-rine

Breaker's Yard

The following cars have to go to the Breaker's Yard. Can the children break the names up into the correct number of syllables? The answers are given in the brackets. Using pictures from car magazines and 'Auto Trader' adds interest to this activity. Cut the pictures of the cars into the same number of pieces as the number of syllables in the car name.

Rover	(2: Ro-ver)	Subaru	(3: Su-ba-ru)
Peugeot	(2: Peu-geot)	Suzuki	(3: Su-zu-ki)
Mini	(2: Min-i)	Land Rover	(3: Land Ro-ver)
Bentley	(2: Bent-ley)	Mitsubishi	(4: Mit-su-bi-shi)
Fiesta	(3: Fi-es-ta)	Alfa Romeo	(5: Al-fa-Ro-me-o)

See also the homework activities on page 16–19

Literacy homework

Name

Return by

Counting Syllables: What to do

1. Look in your fridge or food cupboard and make a list of six things to eat.

2. Count the number of syllables (beats) in each word.

3. Draw pictures of the items.

4. Write the number of syllables next to each one, e.g. 'bread' has 1 beat, and 'apples' has 2.

This work had:

Parent signature/comment

☐ **no help**

☐ **some help**

☐ **a lot of help**

Literacy homework

Name

Return by

Counting Syllables: What to do

You will need a top ten music chart.

1. Write down the name of each performer.

2. Count the number of syllables (beats) in each performer's name, e.g. 'Cold-play' has 2 beats, 'Red-hot-chil-li-pep-pers' has 6.

3. Write the number of syllables next to each name.

This work had: **Parent signature/comment**

☐ no help

☐ some help

☐ a lot of help

Literacy homework

Name

Return by

Blending Syllables: What to do

1. Draw 4 glasses on a sheet of paper.

2. Make up a smoothie flavour for each glass, drawing and colouring in the fruits and other ingredients.

3. Practise saying the separate syllables (beats) in the names of the smoothies, eg 'le-mon' and 'co-co-nut'.

4. Can your friends blend the syllables together to guess the name of the smoothie? Can you blend theirs?

This work had:

☐ no help

☐ some help

☐ a lot of help

Parent signature/comment

Literacy homework

Name

Return by

Segmenting syllables: What to do

You will need some old magazines.

1. Draw or cut out pictures of 6 different types of car from magazines.

2. Stick these onto paper and write down the make of the car next to the picture.

3. Write down the number of syllables (beats) in each name by the pictures, eg 'Fi-es-ta' has 3 beats.

This work had: **Parent signature/comment**

☐ no help

☐ some help

☐ a lot of help

Recognising Rhyme

Fun in the Sun

Help the pupils find these holiday places on a map. Say the names of the places and ask them to listen carefully to the ending of the words.

France	Greece	Rome	Venice
Malta	Spain	Crete	Fife
Wales	Devon	Kerry	

Then ask them to listen to this list of words and identify which words rhyme with the holiday places.

train	tennis	altar	merry
dance	home	peace	life
heaven	sails	heat	

Use the pairs of words to make rhyming couplets to describe a holiday. For example 'Have the time of your life, In the sunshine in Fife.' Make a class display of the couplets and pictures from travel brochures that illustrate the rhymes.

Greetings Cards

Look at a range of greetings cards with rhyming verses inside, e.g. Birthday, Christmas, Valentine and Get well cards. Read the verses out loud to the pupils and ask them to identify the words that rhyme. Now read out the rhyming couplets below and ask the pupils to decide which type of card they come from.

Hip Hip Hooray!	Mince pies and holly	You're so fine	This little letter,
It's your special day!	Let's all be jolly!	Please be mine.	Is to make you better.

Identify which type of card the following words might belong to and make a list of rhyming words for each one – snow, heart, blue, cake, old, cheer, bad, true. Which rhyming pairs would make good rhymes for greetings cards? Which ones wouldn't?

See also the homework activities on page 22–5

Recognising Alliteration

Fabulous Footie!

Make a list of names of towns and cities that have football teams and apply an alliterative word to each one, creating new names for the clubs. A few examples are given below. Remember to keep it friendly!

- Manchester Marvels
- Sheffield Shiners
- Ipswich Imps
- Nottingham Nippers

Write each team name on a strip of paper highlighting the initial consonant/s. Use the strips to carry out a draw to create a fixtures list.

Make a score table for the list and add fantasy scores. Practise reading out the results as a sports commentator would!

Crispy Crackers

Look at a selection of crisp packets and discuss the different flavours and the initial sounds the names begin with.

Make a list of flavours, e.g. chicken, tomato, salted, and create new exciting product names for the crisp flavours using words that alliterate, e.g. chewy chicken, tangy tomato, spicy salted, saucy sausage, pickled pepper. The flavours can be nice or nasty!

See also the homework activities on page 22–5

Make new labels for the crisp packets and stick them over the original names. Display the packets on the wall. Try the same activity with other food types such as cereals and soups.

Literacy homework

Name

Return by

Recognising Rhyme: What to do

Choose one of the holiday rhymes from your class work.

1. Use the rhyme to make a holiday poster for a travel agent's window. Write the rhyme on the poster and illustrate the rhyme.

2. Add some more holiday rhymes to the poster if you can, for example, 'Have fun in the sun' 'Be cool in the pool!'

This work had: **Parent signature/comment**

☐ no help

☐ some help

☐ a lot of help

Literacy homework

Name

Return by

Recognising Rhyme: What to do

1. Choose a type of greetings card, for example, Get Well, Birthday, Christmas, Divali.

2. Can you make a list of some rhyming words that might go inside the card? For example, a card to welcome people to a new house might use the words – home/roam, start/heart, door/before, key/see, you/new

This work had: **Parent signature/comment**

☐ no help

☐ some help

☐ a lot of help

Literacy homework

Name

Return by

Words that begin with the same sound: What to do

1. Choose a football team.

2. Make up some fantasy names for the players in the team. They can be based on real players or you can make up your own. Make sure the names begin with the same sound, not just the same letter. Here are some suggestions **B**rilliant **B**eckham, **S**corer **S**coles

This work had:

☐ no help

☐ some help

☐ a lot of help

Parent signature/comment

Literacy homework

Name

Return by

Words that begin with the same sound: What to do

1. Try and make up four new flavours for crisps that have not been used before. Make sure the names of the crisps begin with the same initial sound not just the same letter. Here are some suggestions – **ch**illi **ch**eese, **c**urried **c**ustard, **p**ickled **p**izza!

2. Make some labels for the new crisp packets.

This work had: **Parent signature/comment**

☐ no help

☐ some help

☐ a lot of help

Blending and Segmenting Onset and Rime

Animal Antics

Photocopy the animal pictures that are included on the next page (dog, hen, sheep, cat, fly, bear, cow, mouse, pig, horse). Cut them out and then cut each one into two. Shuffle the pieces and place the muddled up pieces around the room.

Without the children knowing, select three of the animals. Choose six children to play the game. Whisper the onset of the first animal name to one child, the onset of the second animal name to another and the third to another child. Now whisper a different one of each of the corresponding rimes to each of the remaining three children.

On the command of 'Animal Antics' the children should move around the room repeating their onset or rime until they find a partner that enables them to make one of the animal names. They should then find the two parts of the animal picture put them together and make the appropriate animal noise! The rest of the group should try to guess the original onsets and rimes they were given.

What's in a name?

Choose some first names with only one syllable, e.g. Tom, Sam. Practise saying the names and then segmenting them into their onsets and rimes, e.g. T-om, S-am. Write the names on cards (an example list is included for you below). Cut the words up into onsets and rimes with scissors. Shuffle the pieces of paper and then try to put them together again.

Cath, Pam, Ken, Tim, Jill, Yaz, Pat, Dan, Gus, Josh, Kate, Steve

This activity can be extended to names with two syllables, but is a much more difficult task, e.g. Kayleigh has a pattern of one onset, one rime, one onset and one rime e.g. K-ay l-eigh, Andrew on the other hand, because it starts with a vowel, has this pattern – one rime, one onset, one rime e.g. An-dr-ew. If you are going to work with two syllable names, break the name into its syllables first and then break each syllable into its onset and rime.

See also the homework activities on page 28–9

Animal Antics

Literacy homework

Name

Return by

Breaking words into onsets and rimes: What to do

1. Choose different 'food and drink' words that only have one syllable (beat).

2. Write the words in big letters on separate pieces of paper. Now cut each word into its onset (beginning consonant/s) and rime (vowel and ending).

Bread is /br/ /ead/.
Toast is /t/ /oast/.
Cheese is /ch/ /eese/.

3. Try and do six of these. Practise saying the words in their two parts.

4. Mix up all the bits of paper. Can you put the words together again?

This work had: **Parent signature/comment**

☐ no help

☐ some help

☐ a lot of help

Literacy homework

Name   Return by

Blending onsets and rimes into words: What to do

1. Write these beginnings of words (onsets) on 8 separate pieces of paper

   sl   fr   f   b   sn   b   m   gr

2. Now write these word endings (rimes) on 8 more bits of paper

   ub   oth   ee   ail   ird   ox   og   ug

3. Ask someone at home to help you read them. Can you put them together to make the names of animals you can find in a garden or park?

4. Stick the bits of paper together and draw a picture of the animal next to each finished word.

This work had: **Parent signature/comment**

☐ **no help**

☐ **some help**

☐ **a lot of help**

Phonemes, Beginning, Middle and End

These activities follow on from Concepts About Print page 7. The learner may need some revision of this before beginning. Remember this is a listening activity; the learners should not be able to see the words. They should also only be working with letter sounds they already know. It may take several weeks for some learners to work through all of these stages.

Working with words

1. The teacher says a whole word made up of three letter sounds and then says the **separated sequence** of letter sounds within that word e.g. 'cat is c-a-t' for the pupil to hear. Help the pupil identify which sound is at the beginning/middle/end. After hearing the list of three sounds, the pupil should be shown three corresponding plastic letters and how these are placed in order on a sequencing board (see page 66). Repeat with other three letter words made from the letter sounds the learner knows.
2. The teacher says a word with three phonemes e.g. 'cat' – **stretching** the sounds out as the word is said. The pupil is shown the three corresponding plastic letters for the word. The pupil says which sound is at the beginning and selects the right plastic letter placing it in the right place on the sequencing board.
3. The teacher says a three letter word, **stretching** the sounds out as the word is said. The pupil says which sound is at the end and puts the corresponding plastic letter in the right place on the sequencing board.
4. The teacher says a three letter word, **stretching** the sounds out as the word is said. The pupil says which sound is in the middle and puts the corresponding plastic letter in the right place on the sequencing board.
5. The teacher says a three letter word with **no stretching**. The pupil says which sound is at the beginning and puts the plastic letter in the right place on the sequencing board.
6. The teacher says a three letter word with **no stretching**. The pupil says which sound is at the end and puts the right plastic letter on the sequencing board.
7. The teacher says a three letter word with **no stretching**. The pupil says which sound is in the middle and puts the right plastic letter on the sequencing board.
8. The teacher says a three letter word with **no stretching**. The pupil segments the three sounds in sequence and places the plastic letters on the sequencing board.

Blending and Segmenting Phonemes

Cyber Speak

Seat the class in a circle to represent a flying saucer. Explain that an alien robot has crash landed on planet earth. People have tried to teach him their names but he speaks in a strange robotic way. Say the names of the children in the group by speaking the individual phonemes in sequence with one second intervals between each phoneme, eg. J-o-sh, Kh-a-l-i-d, A-l-i, M-a-x-i-ne. Make sure you are making the sounds of the phonemes, for example Ali will be pronounced /a/ /l/ /ee/. Ask the children to listen to way the robot says the names and work out who he means.

Explain that the robot is having difficulty learning the names of things around the room. Can the children work out which objects he is trying to name?

sh-oo (shoe)

b-ă-g (bag)

p-ě-n (pen)

g-l-ă-s (glass)

c-l-ŏ-k (clock)

d-ě-s-k (desk)

sh-ě-l-f (shelf)

w-ĭ-n-d-ō (window)

r-ŭ-b-ĭ-sh (rubbish)

p-ě-n-s-ĭ-l (pencil)

c-r-ā-ŏ-n-z (crayons)

j-ă-k-ě-t (jacket)

Cyber Wars

'Segmenter' is a very strong robot. It can break all other robots into pieces with its terrible jaws. It likes to break the robots into the same number of pieces as there are sounds in their names. See if the children are as strong as 'Segmenter' and can do the same with these robots. The answers are given in brackets.

See also the homework activities on page 32–3

Zat (Z-a-t) (3)

Rip (R-i-p) (3)

Cog (C-o-g) (3)

Canz (C-a-n-z) (4)

Bolt (B-o-l-t) (4)

Slick (S-l-i-k) (4)

Crunchup (C-r-u-n-ch-u-p) (7)

Busta (B-u-s-t-a) (5)

Teckno (T-e-k-n-o) (5)

Fliplip (F-l-i-p-l-i-p) (7)

Manick (M-a-n-i-k) (5)

Tinpet (T-i-n-p-e-t) (6)

Gadjet (G-a-d-j-e-t) (6)

Pushkin (P-u-sh-k-i-n) (6)

Thundrex (Th-u-n-d-r-e-k-s) (8)

Literacy homework

| Name | Return by |

Breaking words into sounds: What to do

Robodust is a house robot who has come to do the dusting at your house. He is learning to talk and can only speak one sound at a time. When Robodust dusts the bin, he says the three sounds b-i-n.

1. Think of six things Robodust can dust.

2. Draw a picture of Robodust and the things he has dusted.

3. Practise saying the names of the things you have drawn like Robodust, one sound at a time.

4. Test your friends and see if they can listen to the sounds and work out what Robodust has dusted.

This work had:

☐ no help

☐ some help

☐ a lot of help

Parent signature/comment

Literacy homework

Name

Return by

Blending sounds into words: What to do

1. Can you blend these sounds together to make up some names for aliens?

Z-o-g   T-i-j   G-u-p

P-l-e-k   S-e-z-i-t   H-i-p-u-t-z

2. Now can you work out the names of these strange planets?

P-a-v-o-n   N-e-sh   Z-i-n-t

D-r-o-t   L-e-f-i-b   J-e-t-i-l

3. Choose one of the aliens to draw. What do you think it looks like? Which one of the planets does it come from? What is it like there?

This work had:

☐ no help

☐ some help

☐ a lot of help

Parent signature/comment

Alphabet and Dictionary Skills

Knowledge of the alphabet is essential for communicating through written language and mastery of alphabetic order is needed for many reference and modern communication systems. As a comparatively recent example of this, look at how important the use of the mobile phone and e-mail is to popular culture and consider how much the simple act of texting or e-mailing a friend relies on alphabetic knowledge.

Some learners gain these skills easily, for others it can take much longer; little and often is the key. In literacy learning, letter names remain constant, so there can be a real sense of achievement in mastering them. Once learned they are a clear and unambiguous reference point for the teacher and learner in their future work together.

If learners have to keep going back to 'A' to work out a letter or to establish alphabetic order, they do not know their alphabet efficiently.

Mastering the alphabet has five main different aspects:

1. Identifying and naming the letter shapes and their correct orientation
2. A speedy recall of alphabetic order and an individual letter's position within this
3. Moving confidently and efficiently forwards and backwards through the alphabet
4. Knowing how alphabetic order can help us search for and organise information
5. Applying this to real life activities through creating and using alphabets

However, it is important that these skills should not be seen as a hierarchy to be moved through one at a time nor should learning the alphabet be seen as an end in itself. Real life application is essential at all stages of learning.

Leading Activities

Before you start

Look back to page 13 to remind yourself of the need to keep the terms 'letter' and 'sound' distinct from each other. Remember in this section we are concerned with the letter names and not the sounds they represent. Insist on this terminology from your pupils.

Which style of letters?

The physical movement and orientation of letter shapes is essential to multi-sensory learning. Use wooden, plastic or magnetic letters, rather than alphabet cards, but be mindful of age appropriateness. Both lower and upper case need to be used, but use only one case initially, matching the other case to this once it has been learned. Later, take time to study the different fonts that word processors can use or the artistic forms letters can take in print making and calligraphy.

Alphabet and dictionary skills

Layout

Encourage your learners to lay their letters out from A–Z in the shape of an arc or a rainbow towards the top of the table you are working on. This means that all the letters are in one line and can be accessed easily. The letter M should be at the mid-point.

Teach the alphabet in four sections

First – ABCD
Second – EFGHIJKLM
Third – NOPQR
Fourth – STUVWXYZ

A standard dictionary can be divided into four sections which are roughly equal; knowing these helps with ease of reference when moving through a dictionary. The sections are referred to as 'quartiles' (see Hickey 2001). The quartiles relate to the number of pages they contain, not the number of letters they refer to. Some letters have many more words than others and therefore more pages. Dictionaries vary, so check out the one you will be using first and amend the quartiles if necessary.

Apply to real life situations

Practise the five different aspects of alphabet work mentioned on page 36 in different contexts. The emphasis you place on the text types will depend on the age of your pupil.

Try using alphabetic lists, indexes in information books, shopping catalogues, library catalogues, databases, business directories and the 'Yellow Pages', telephone directories, web sites, address books including mobile phones and e-mail, texting and alphabets relating to personal interests.

Dictionary skills

Teach finding a word using the first letter to begin with, adapting your materials and lists accordingly. Introduce second letter skills once first letter skills are being used comparatively efficiently. When using real life contexts, the need to use at least the second letter in alphabet work quickly becomes apparent. Spend time teaching this as an additional skill. Do not assume your pupil will understand that words are organised alphabetically through their second letters too.

Alphabet Activities

Use shaped letters or alphabet cards for the following activities.

Alphabet sequencing

- Matching a set of letters to an existing alphabet sequence
- Using an alphabet book as a guide to laying out the sequence
- Ordering the alphabet in four sections (see page 37)
- Ordering the whole alphabet
- Ordering the alphabet without frequent return to 'a', teach returns to the letters at the beginning of the alphabet quartiles instead (see page 37)

Identifying letters

- Identifying individual letters pointed to within an alphabet sequence
- Guessing the missing letter/s from an alphabet sequence
- Identifying random letters that are out of sequence

Reciting the alphabet

- Saying the alphabet with a partner, alternating letters, first saying one letter each, then two or three
- Saying which letter comes next or before a letter that you name, first with the alphabet in view, then without
- Saying the alphabet in different rhythms

Increasing fluency

- Increasing the speed of laying out the letters through timing the activity with a stop watch, encourage improvement on personal best

Alphabet and dictionary skills

Different fonts

- Matching lower case letters to an upper case alphabet
- Matching different fonts of the same letter

Preparing for dictionary work

- Matching pictures or objects to an alphabet
- Ordering a set of pictures alphabetically
- Generating a spoken list of words in alphabetic order, using a theme, e.g. types of food, makes of car
- Rearranging a short list of spoken words into an alphabetic sequence
- Use alphabet books, dictionaries or directories to find specified first letters
- Putting small groups of letters into alphabetic order e.g. fksil-fikls
- Putting a set of word cards into alphabetic order
- Identify which direction to go within an alphabet book to find the next specified letter

See also the homework activities on page 49–51

About the Alphabet Masters

The next three pages of upper case and lower case letters and corresponding picture clues for the alphabet can be copied and used in a variety of ways. The following suggestions may be helpful.

Lotto

Any one of the three masters can be used as a base board, and then a second copy can be cut into separate cards to match on top. The matching cards can be of the same case, or, for example, lower case letters could be matched to upper case, or the letters could be matched to the picture clues. This enables the same sets to be used in a variety of ways.

Card games

If the masters are cut into individual pieces then 'Snap' and 'Pairs' can be played, matching cards in the same variety of ways as described above.

Board games

Games such as snakes and ladders can be used alongside the cards, with learners having to identify alphabet letters to enable them to go up a ladder or to save them from sliding down a snake. Learners can make their own versions of such games where instead of the traditional snakes and ladders, other motifs can be used, such as skate boards going up and down ramps or rockets taking off and descending.

Pot of Gold (page 44) is an alphabet game for two players that practises alphabetic order and the rainbow layout.

Upper and Lower Case Match (page 45) helps learners recognise both type faces.

Using a Dictionary (page 46) involves finding words in a dictionary and putting them into alphabetic order.

Which way next? (page 47) is a teacher-led activity that improves efficiency in moving through a dictionary.

Make a Fashion Catalogue (page 48) extends the use of alphabetic order to indexes.

See also the homework activities on page 49–51

Alphabet Master 1: Lower case letters

a	<u>b</u>	c	<u>d</u>
e	f	g	h
i	j	k	l
m	<u>n</u>	o	<u>p</u>
q	r	s	t
<u>u</u>	v	w	x
y	z		

Alphabet Master 2: Capital letters

A	B	C	D
E	F	G	H
I	J	K	L
M	N	O	P
Q	R	S	T
U	V	W	X
Y	Z		

Alphabet and dictionary skills

Alphabet Master 3: Picture clues

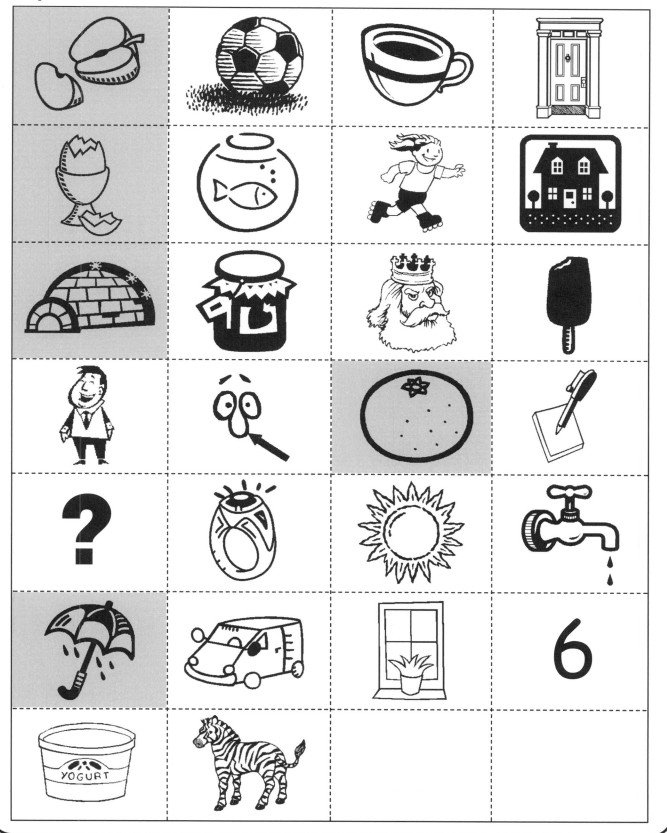

Alphabetic Order

Pot of Gold

- Can you put your letters in a rainbow shape like this?

- Check your alphabet with this one.

abcdefghijklmnopqrstuvwxyz

- Now make a pot like this and some gold coins.

- Play the Pot of Gold game with a friend.
- Ask your friend to close his or her eyes.
- Now hide a letter in the rainbow with the pot of gold.
- Can your friend say which letter is under the gold?
- Give them a gold coin or a counter if they get it right.
- Take it in turns to play the game.

Alphabet and dictionary skills

Upper and lower case match

Can you write the lower case letter next to each capital?

A__	B__	C__	D__
E__	F__	G__	H__
I__	J__	K__	L__
M__	N__	O__	P__
Q__	R__	S__	T__
U__	V__	W__	X__
Y__	Z__		

Using a Dictionary

- Can you find these words in the dictionary?
- Write the word under the picture.

_____	_____	_____	_____

- Now find these words.
- Draw the picture to go with the word.

rat	map	van	jam

- Cut out all the words and pictures you have found and put them in alphabetic order.

Dictionary Skills: Which Way Next?

Using First Letter Knowledge

Each player will need a dictionary and two large cards, one that says 'turn on' and another that says 'go back'. It may also be helpful to have arrows on the cards indicating the direction to turn.

Write the word 'window' on the board with a picture clue if needed. Ask everyone to find 'window' in their dictionary and to keep the page open once they have found it.

Now write the word 'door' on the board. Ask the players to predict which way they will have to turn the pages to go from 'window' to 'door'. They should hold up a card indicating their choice before finding the new word.

Continue with further words appropriate to players' interests and abilities.

Second Letter knowledge

Play the game in the same way to practise the use of second letter clues. Initially work within one letter section at a time such as 'b'. It is helpful to put bookmarks at the start and end of 'b' to limit the search or to paper clip the section open. Ask the players to predict which way they will turn when looking for bat, box, big, belt, banana, etc. Make sure the examples you give only require second letter knowledge; for example, moving from 'bird' to 'biscuit' is more advanced and needs third letter skills.

See also the homework activities on page 49–51

Indexes: Make a fashion catalogue

Look at a fashion catalogue. Use the index at the back to help you find

- some jeans
- a hat
- a coat
- a t-shirt
- and some boots.

Now make your own catalogue with an index.

1. First make a set of 6 pictures of different types of clothing. You could use pictures from magazines, clip art, or you could draw them.
2. Put each item of clothing on a separate page and write a sentence describing it underneath.
3. Put the names of the types of clothes into alphabetic order and order your pages in the same way.
4. Number the pages.
5. Make an index for the back of your catalogue.
6. Finally make a cover for the catalogue and clip all the pages together.
7. Share the catalogue with a friend.

Literacy homework

Name

Return by

Knowing which direction to turn the pages in a dictionary: What to do

You will need a dictionary for this game.

1. Find the first word in the box – man.

2. Which way do you have to turn to find the next word – leg?

3. Draw the arrow on the line to say which way.

4. Find the second word.

man	bin	sun	cup
———	———	———	———
leg	fish	nut	well

This work had: **Parent signature/comment**

☐ no help

☐ some help

☐ a lot of help

Literacy homework

Name

Return by

Putting words into alphabetic order: What to do

Can you put these names into alphabetic order for the address book in a mobile phone? Practise reading the names and make them into a list.

Tom, Ben, Kath, Liz, Val, Pat, Jan, Sam, Nick, Fran, Yap, Mel

This work had: **Parent signature/comment**

[ ] no help

[ ] some help

[ ] a lot of help

Literacy homework

Name

Return by

Learning the alphabet: What to do

You will need:
A set of alphabet letters and a copy of 'Pot of Gold'

Play the pot of gold game with someone at home.

This work had: **Parent signature/comment**

☐ no help

☐ some help

☐ a lot of help

Letter Sound Links

A Multi-sensory Structured Approach

A carefully structured multi-sensory approach to letter–sound correspondence is essential, where the learner is using and developing visual, oral, auditory and kinaesthetic skills.

looking

speaking

hearing

doing

In a multi-sensory approach the learner is asked to combine

- looking carefully at letter shapes and patterns, their sequence within words, studying their salient features
- saying the letter sounds and words out aloud, feeling the 'sound shape' in the mouth and throat as it is spoken
- hearing the letter sounds and their 'auditory position' within words – does the sound come at the beginning, the middle or the end?
- writing or moving letters shapes into their 'physical position' within a sequence, feeling the shape of the letter patterns and words through the hands and body

Teaching New Letter Sounds

As each new letter sound is taught the learner should be asked to listen to a word that begins with the target sound, say the whole word and then say the initial sound they can hear. Can they identify any other words that begin or end with that sound? The initial sound should then be linked to the appropriate letter shape so that the learner can see the lower case, upper case and handwritten form. The learner should then be taught how to write the letter correctly, learning its formation, position on the line, height and how it is joined to other letters.

A Teaching Order

The checklist on page 56–7 suggests an order for the learning of
- Letter names and sounds
- Useful rimes
- High and Medium Frequency words

It can be used to record both teaching (t) and mastery (m). Dated records will also show a learner's rate of progress.

Letter sound links

Letter names and sounds

The teaching order is progressive. As the learners work down the first two columns on the left they gradually build up their knowledge of letter names and their corresponding sounds. Each letter sound has a clue word and picture which aids discrimination, pronunciation and recall of the letter sound link. Pictures for the clue words are on pages 60 and 62.

At each new point in the order, the learner is asked to use the new letter sound that has been taught in both reading and spelling activities, but is only asked to do this with words that are made up of the set of letter sounds that have been covered so far.

Differentiation

The letter sound checklist can be used at different levels.

> **Level One** – single consonant sounds, short vowel sounds and consonant digraphs
> **Level Two** – further consonant blends, endings and spelling choices (listed in italics)

Some learners respond best by working at level one and then returning to the consonant blends later. Other learners are ready to work with letter blends straight away.

Useful Rimes

As the letter sounds are acquired they are then combined into useful word endings (rimes) for reading and spelling phonically regular words.

High and Medium Frequency Words

Words from the National Literacy Strategy are also introduced in a structured way. These are divided into High frequency 1, High frequency 2 and Medium frequency words. Again, use of these will depend on the learner's needs.

The NLS words are arranged within the checklist to correspond with the teaching order for letter sounds; each word consists only of letters that have been learned so far. In this way all the letters within a word will be visually familiar to the learner and can be named.

Words that have similar visual patterns within each section have also been grouped together. Bracketed words contain consonant digraphs and are optional. They are repeated later in the list once that digraph has been taught.

As most of the NLS words are too complex for phonic analysis at this stage or are irregular, it is suggested that these are learned through a visual approach. Use the word learning routine described on pages 122–3. (For a more detailed multisensory approach to teaching and learning using this letter and word order refer to Broomfield and Combley 2003)

Letter sound links

Letter Sound Checklist 1. Name   Date

Letter name	Picture clue and sound	t	m	Useful rimes	High frequency 1	High frequency 2	Medium frequency
i	igloo /i/				I		
t	tap /t/			it	it		
p	pen /p/			ip			
n	nose /n/			in	in		
s	sun /s/			is	is		
st	*stone /st/*						
sp	*spider /sp/*						
sn	*snail /sn/*						
a	apple /a/			at ap	at	as an	
d	door /d/			id ad and	and said dad	did	didn't
h	house /h/				this	his has had (than) (that)	
e	egg /e/			et en est ent end	the he she see	seen (then) (these)	head inside
c	cup /k/				can cat	can't	
k	king /k/			ick eck ack ask esk		take	asked (think)
ck							
sk	*skip /sk/*						
c or k							
b	ball /b/			ab		bed be been back	
r	ring /r/				are	her here ran	better heard
br	*bread /br/*					sister tree	near paper
cr	*cry /cr/*					(there) (their)	started tries
dr	*drum /dr/*					(three)	(earth)
pr	*present /pr/*						
tr	*tree /tr/*						
m	man /m/			im am amp	me am	came him made make man name time (them)	I'm
sm	*smarties /sm/*						
y	yogurt /y/				(they) my yes day	by many may	any baby eyes happy birthday year
l	lolly /l/			all ell ill	like play all	ball call called help last little	animals lady place small still (children)
bl	*blanket /bl/*						
cl	*cloud /c/*						
pl	*plate /pl/*						
sl	*slide /sl/*						
f	fish /f/					if after first half	different (father) friends
fl	*flower /fl/*						
fr	*frog /fr/*						

Letter sound links

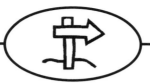

Letter Sound Checklist 2. Name   Date

Letter name	Picture clue and sound	t	m	Useful rimes	High frequency 1	High frequency 2	Medium frequency
o	orange /o/			ot od op ock ost	of to on no look for	(another) boy do don't door from home more not off old once or people school so some too took	across almost also balloon before (both) (clothes) does important money (mother) only often opened sometimes stopped today told
g **gl** **gr**	girl /g/ glove /gl/ grass /gr/			ag eg ig og	go going dog big get	again dig girl good got night	along began being (change) coming garden goes gone great high light might right morning (together) (something)
u	umbrella /u/			un u gut u bull ump	you up mum	about because but could out us (push) must your (should) pull cut house laugh (much) (much)	found round sound around such suddenly sure turn turned under until upon used (through) (thought) brought young during number outside
j	jam /j /					just jump	jumped
v	van /v/					have over very love loved live lived	above every leave never
w **sw** **tw**	window /w/ swim /sw/ twins /tw/				was away we went	down how now new saw two want water way were would will (who) (with) (what) (when) (where)	always between write walked know show own window below following woke woken swimming (why) (whole) (while) (white) (without)
x	six (ks)			ax ex ix ox		next	
z	zebra /z/						
qu	question /kw/						
th	thin /th /			ath	the this they	that than there their them then these three with brother	birthday both clothes earth father mother other those thought through together without
sh	shop /sh/			ash ish ush	she	push should	show
ch **tch**	chips /ch/ match /tch/			atch itch utch		much	change children such watch
wh	wheel /wh/					what when where who	why while whole white
ng	sting /ng/			ang ing ong ung			along during being coming following morning something swimming young
nk	sink /nk/			ank ink unk			think

Building a Memory Pack

Making the cards

New letter sounds should be taught one at a time, in the order given in the checklist on page 56–7. As each new letter sound is introduced it is linked to a memory card. White cards are used for consonants, blue cards for vowels.

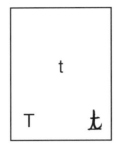 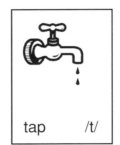

In the middle of the front of the card is the printed letter/s of the sound that is to be learned. In the bottom left corner is the upper case form and in the bottom right corner is the joined form. On the back of the card is a picture of a clue word for that letter sound along with the sound clue and the written word.

Learners can make their own cards or they can be given one from the master sets on pages 60–3. Making the card for themselves is usually an enjoyable activity and gives further opportunity to use kinaesthetic skills within a multisensory approach. As the learner progresses, a whole pack of cards will be acquired that can be used for word reading and spelling.

Rehearsing the pack

Rehearsal of the memory pack should be a regular feature of lessons. At the beginning of each lesson, the learner should be asked to look at the letter form on the front of each card and 'say their cards' in the following way.

'tap' (recalling the picture clue on the back and
saying a word that begins with the letter sound)

't' (isolating the appropriate sound)

'tee' (naming the letter)

The learner should then check on the back of the card to see if they were correct. This soon builds into a familiar routine and allows for frequent rehearsal and 'over learning' of the letter sounds.

Letter sound links

Laying out the cards

After the cards have been rehearsed they should be set out on the table in a line above the sequencing board (see page 66) and the learner's writing book or paper. To begin with the cards can be set out in any order; as more cards are collected, they can then be put out alphabetically. The memory cards are then ready to be used for reading and spelling words as described on pages 64–5.

Using the Letter Sound Masters

Master sets of the letter sounds and their corresponding clue words are provided. These can be copied and made into memory cards.

Master 1 –   picture clues and their corresponding sounds at level one

Master 2 –   letter forms for the above, lower case, upper case and handwritten cursive

The two masters should be photocopied back to back, cut into individual cards and then laminated. The front of each card has the letter form on, the back the picture and sound clue.

Master 3 –   picture clues and their corresponding sounds at level two

Master 4 –   letter forms for the above, lower case, upper case and handwritten cursive

Master three and four should be photocopied back to back and made into individual cards as for the previous set.

Letter sound links

Master 1: Single Sounds – Picture Clues

apple /a/	ball /b/	cup /k/	door /d/
egg /e/	fish /f/	girl /g/	house /h/
igloo /i/	jam /j/	king /k/	lolly /l/
man /m/	nose /n/	orange /o/	pen /p/
question /kw/	ring /r/	sun /s/	tap /t/
umbrella /u/	van /v/	window /w/	six /ks/
yoghurt /y/	zebra /z/		

Letter sound links

Master 2: Single Sounds – Letters

d	c	b	a
D *d*	C *c*	B *b*	A *a*
h	g	f	e
H *h*	G *g*	F *f*	E *e*
l	k	j	i
L *l*	K *k*	J *j*	I *i*
p	o	n	m
P *p*	O *o*	N *n*	M *m*
t	s	r	qu
T *t*	S *s*	R *r*	QU *qu*
x	w	v	u
X *x*	W *w*	V *v*	U *u*
		z	y
		Z *z*	Y *y*

Master 3: Blends and Digraphs – Picture Clues

shop /sh/	thin /th/	chips /ch/	wheel /wh/
sting /ng/	sink /nk/	stone /st/	spider /sp/
snail /sn/	skip /sk/	bread /br/	cry /cr/
drum /dr/	present /pr/	tree /tr/	smarties /sm/
blanket /bl/	cloud /cl/	plate /pl/	slide /sl/
flower /fl/	frog /fr/	gloves /gl/	grass /gr/
swim /sw/	twins /tw/		

Letter sound links

Master 4: Blends and Digraphs – Letters

wh	ch	th	sh
WH *wh*	CH *ch*	TH *th*	SH *sh*
sp	st	nk	ng
SP *sp*	ST *st*	NK *nk*	NG *ng*
cr	br	sk	sn
CR *cr*	BR *br*	SK *sk*	SN *sn*
sm	tr	pr	dr
SM *sm*	TR *tr*	PR *pr*	DR *dr*
sl	pl	cl	bl
SL *sl*	PL *pl*	CL *cl*	BL *bl*
gr	gl	fr	fl
GR *gr*	GL *gl*	FR *fr*	FL *fl*
		tw	sw
		TW *tw*	SW *sw*

Reading and Spelling Words

Using a Sequencing Board

The cards from the memory pack are used with a sequencing board (page 66) to blend sounds together for reading and to segment words for spelling. This can be used at any point or level in the teaching programme and is an essential part of the multi-sensory learning routine described on page 54.

The memory cards are placed onto the board in a left to right sequence. Wooden or plastic letters may also be used. The white space at the beginning or end of the board is for single consonants (e.g. s) or consonant blends (e.g. st) or digraphs (e.g. sh). The coloured space in the middle is for the short vowel sounds (a e i o u) and should be coloured blue to match the vowel cards.

When using the board, it is important that the learners should be asked to work only with letter sounds that have been covered so far. Each time a new letter sound is added to their learning pack it can be used for spelling and reading words as described below. Use the checklist on pages 56–7 to help structure this process.

Reading words

The teacher places letter sounds that make up a whole word on the board, but does not read it; the learner decodes the word, working from left to right. The learner then reads the whole word aloud and writes it down. Verbal sentences containing the word can also be composed to ensure that the word is understood.

Differentiation

This approach can be used at the different levels described below.

Working at level 1

(single consonants and short vowels)

A group of words with the same rime can be read in this way to emphasize the letter pattern and sound similarities. Use the rimes listed within the checklist on pages 56–7 to structure and pace their introduction.

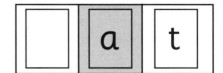

Note that words that start with a vowel (e.g. at) should begin on the blue space, the preceding white space will be empty.

Working at level 2

(consonant blends and digraphs and short vowel sounds)

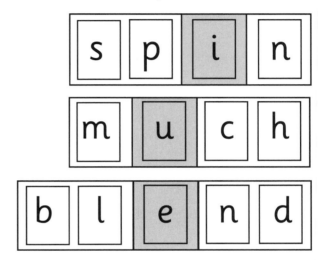

- initial blends or digraph

- final blends or digraph

- using both initial and final blends

Spelling words

The sequencing board and letters are used in a similar way for spelling, but this time the teacher says a whole word to the learner first, such as 'pat'. The learner then has to segment the word into its three sounds, find the correct letters and place them in left to right order on the board. Having made the word correctly, it should then be read back and written down.

Again **it is essential that the learner should be asked to work only with letter sounds that have been learned so far**.

Spelling groups of words with the same rime helps the learner begin to make analogies. The teacher can encourage this through saying, for example, 'Now that you have made the word 'cat', how can you change it into the word 'pat?' What is the same about the two words? What is different? What other word could you make that has the same pattern at the end?'

Working with Two Syllable Words see Chapter 5.

Letter sound links

Master for Sequencing Boards

Beginning, Middle, End

beginning	middle	end

Word Building

consonants	vowel	consonants

Working with Sentences

Sentence Dictation

Sentences dictated by the teacher are an important part of the learning programme; they are a significant step towards independent writing. The learner has to work with all the different skills that have been taught in an integrated way.

A letter sound is not truly mastered until it is used correctly within sentences and then independently in free writing. At first learners may use the sequencing board for working out each individual word, but as they progress it will need to be used only for words that they are unsure of or for making corrections.

Work with the known

When choosing a sentence for dictation include only high frequency words and letter sounds that are already known. For example, by letter 'd' in the checklist on page 56 the sentence 'Pat hid his hat.' could be made, but the sentence 'Ted hid his hat.' could not be used until after the letter 'e' has been taught.

Include Punctuation

Working with dictated sentences is an ideal time to work on correct punctuation. The learners can be reminded before dictation begins about the need to include capital letters, full stops and question marks. They will then need to remember this without prompting when writing the sentence down.

A Point System

Including a point system when marking completed sentences increases motivation. Points can be given for whole words that are written correctly, or for individual letters in the right place. The use of bonus points for correct punctuation is an added incentive.

Sentence reading

Make sentences for reading in the same way as for spelling, by restricting the words to high frequency words and letter sounds already known. The learner can match these to pictures you have provided or draw a quick sketch to illustrate the sentence for themselves. Try using cloze sentences where the reader has to fill in a missing word, either independently or from a list of possible answers. Sentences can also be cut up into individual words and then rearranged in the correct order (see page 120) or they can be cut into halves and made into new ones by splicing the two halves from different sentences together.

Integrated Reading and Writing

Pupils following the **Overcoming Dyslexia** programme should also be given the opportunity to take part in the wide range of literacy activities that the National Literacy Strategy has to offer. The classroom handbook for **Overcoming Dyslexia** gives detailed advice on this. The simple techniques and resources suggested here can give further support and help to generalise skills from structured sessions into the classroom.

Using Memory Packs Alongside a Reading Book

Learners' memory packs can be laid out at the top of their table alongside a laminated sequencing board or mini white board and pen. These can be used to work out spellings for classroom writing activities, or to analyse words that cause difficulty when reading.

To Reinforce Letter Sound Links

When a letter sound has been taught, try to find opportunities for the learners to use this in their everyday reading. Give them the appropriate memory card and ask them to scan a text to find examples of the letter sound. Can they say whether the sound comes at the beginning, middle or end of the words that they find?

For Prompting Reading

When readers have difficulty with a word that contains sounds that they have been working on, temporarily isolate it from the text by writing it on a mini white board or building it out of memory cards. Encourage the reader to recall the letter sounds they have covered and if possible to blend these together to help decode the word. Even just deciding on the first few letters or the beginning and the ending may help. Then find the word within the text again and see if the letter sound clues alongside the context enable it to be read successfully. Return to these words again at the end of the reading session. It is obviously important not to overdo this or the enjoyment and sense of the story will be lost. Four or five words a session is sufficient.

Using the Memory Packs when Writing

When writers ask for spellings, encourage them to try and work them out before resorting to a dictionary. Use the sequencing board and memory cards or a white board and marker pen to do this. Ask them to 'stretch' the word (see page 30) and to write down the sounds they hear. Being able to wipe the word away, or move their memory cards often encourages more reluctant spellers to have a go. You can also partly share the spelling with a writer, they write the sounds they know and you fill in the gaps.

Make Desktop Memory Aids

Once a memory pack becomes full, it can be unwieldy. Learners can use laminated A4 desktop prompts instead of separate cards; the masters for these are on pages 69 and 70. The three spaces at the end can be used as a mini sequencing board along with a marker pen. If preferred an alphabet strip can be made from the master and taped to the top of a table instead.

Letter sound links

Desktop Master – Single Sounds

Desktop Master – Blends and Digraphs

sh SH	th TH	ch CH	wh W H
sh	th	ch	wh
ng NG	nk NK	st ST	sp SP
ng	nk	st	sp
sn SN	sk SK	br BR	cr CR
sn	sk	br	cr
dr DR	pr PR	tr TR	sm SM
dr	pr	tr	sm
bl BL	cl CL	pl PL	sl SL
bl	cl	pl	sl
fl FL	fr FR	gl GL	gr GR
fl	fr	gl	gr
		sw SW	tw TW
		sw	tw

Games and Activities

The activity masters on pages 73–5, 81–2 have been kept blank for you to fill in the letter sounds and rimes appropriate for the learners you work with. Use the checklist on pages 56–7 to decide which ones can be used at each stage. The activities can be used individually or with groups and can be used alongside the memory pack and sequencing board routines. Any additional instructions needed for use are given below. All the activities can be played at either level one or level two.

Spin It! page 73

Write an onset in each box and a rime in each section of the spinner.

Word Chains, page 74

This master can be used to make a set of words where each new word in a list begins with the same letter that the previous word ended with, e.g. cat-tap-pen-nut. Pupils can use the master to make up their own chains using their memory cards and sequencing boards to help them. Or the teacher can make a set for them to see if they can turn the words into one continuous chain. Remember to muddle up the words! The word chains can also be cut out and used to play dominoes.

Wordsearch, page 75

This master can either be used by the teacher to create word searches for the learner using words made from the letters they have covered so far, or the learner can create their own for a friend using their memory pack and sequencing board to help them.

Vowel Discrimination List, pages 76–9

Many learners find discrimination between the vowel sounds difficult. Use the list to help you structure games and activities. Words with the same rimes are grouped together.

Select a group of words from the list with two different vowel sounds in the middle, e.g. /i/ or /e/. The learner should not be able to see the words. The teacher should say the words clearly but naturally. The learner listens to each word, selects the right vowel card from their memory pack and places it in the middle of their sequencing board. Points can be awarded for each correct answer.

Odd One Out

Select a set of three words that share the same vowel sound and one that doesn't from the list on pages 76–9. Can the learner spot the odd one out?

Word Pairs and Snap

Use the list to create pairs games or snap where pairs of words that share the same vowel sound can be collected instead of identical words.

Letter sound links

Vowel Cross, pages 80–1

This game is used at level one to build cvc words and at level two to build ccvc or cvcc or ccvcc words within boxes arranged in cross shapes. It is a game for two or three players. Words can only be made from left to right and from top to bottom.

Before you begin, colour the box in the centre of each cross blue to represent the vowel cards in pupil's packs and to give a visual link to their sequencing boards. At this point, you can vary the way the game is played to ensure success or to build in challenge.

Level One

The game can be restricted to using only those cards in a player's own memory pack or for more able players it can be played with a full set of alphabet cards with no picture clues (page 41). Players make cvc words according to the instructions on page 80 and score 3 points for each correct word. The player with the most points at the end is the winner.

Level Two

If played at level two, two letter blends or digraphs can be written in the boxes instead of single letter sounds, thus enabling longer words to be made. Again the play can be restricted to memory packs, or a full set of blends (page 63) can be mixed into an alphabet set. A point is awarded for each letter, thus the player completing the word 'west' would score 4, but 'twist' would score 5 points.

Advanced

For players who need more of a challenge and tactical play, a full set of alphabet cards without picture clues should be used (page 41). Players have to recall consonant blends and digraphs for themselves. As they turn over single consonant cards, these may be held in the hand for later use with other letters to make blends and digraphs at an appropriate time. Players need to remember which letters have already been used (or mark these off on an alphabet line) to ensure that they are not waiting for a card which has already been played. One point is given for each letter in a completed word. Players still holding cards at the end of the game have one point deducted from their score for each letter in their hand. The person with the highest number of points wins.

Top of the Tower, page 82

This is a vowel discrimination game and can be used to discriminate between two to five different vowels. Use the list of words on pages 76–9 to help you. Each player should work with a different vowel sound and have a tower with their vowel on and a counter. The players listen to a list of words said by the teacher. If they correctly hear their vowel sound in the middle of a word, they shout out their sound or letter name. If they are correct they move a counter up the tower or write in the sound or word. The first player to reach the top of the tower is the winner.

See also the homework activities on page 83–5

Spin it!

- Spin the discs and make the words.
- Write the words carefully.

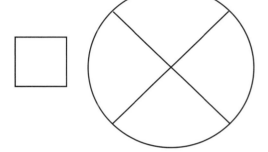

_____ _____ _____

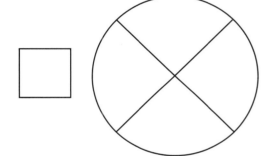

_____ _____ _____

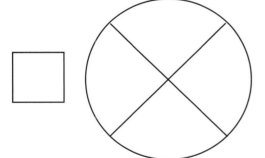

_____ _____ _____

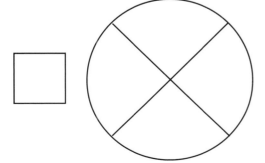

_____ _____ _____

Teacher Instructions on page 71

Word chain

- Cut out the word pairs keeping them inside their link.
- Can you put them together into one long chain?
- Match the last letter in each word with the first letter in the next word.

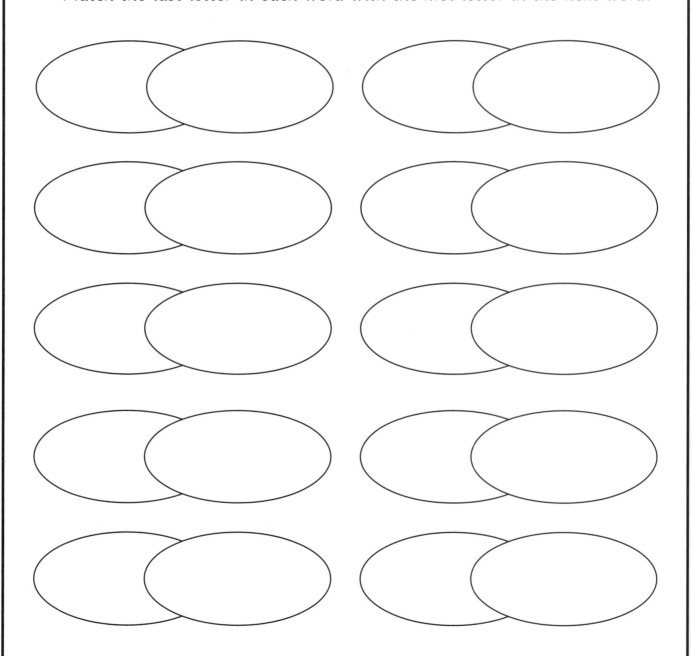

This game can also be played like dominoes.

Teacher Instructions on page 71.

Letter sound links

Wordsearch

Can you find these words in the wordsearch?

_____   _____   _____   _____   _____

_____   _____   _____   _____   _____

_____   _____   _____   _____   _____

Teacher Instructions on page 71.

Vowel Discrimination and Rimes List 1.

The lists of words below have been organised into rime families for ease of reference and into two levels. Level one has single consonants plus ck, ss and ll; level two words contain consonant blends, digraphs and some trigraphs. All the words have short vowel sounds for the author, but some speakers will find otherwise due to their regional pronunciation. The word lists can be used to support rhyming activities, spelling analogies, vowel discrimination, and Top of the Tower on page 82.

ĭ Level one	rib, fib, bib,	kid, bid, rid, did, lid, quid, hid, mid, Sid	pig, tig, dig, big, rig, fig, wig, jig, gig,
lick, pick, tick, quick, kick, Mick, Rick, Dick, nick, sick	six, fix, mix	till, pill, sill, hill, kill, bill, Bill, mill, fill, gill, Jill, will, quill,	Tim, him, dim, rim, Jim, Kim,
in, win, pin, quin, din, bin, fin, kin, sin, tin	dip, hip, tip, nip, lip, rip, dip, zip, kip, pip, sip, quip	hiss, kiss, miss,	it, pit, sit, hit, kit, bit, lit, fit, quit, wit, nit, zit

ĭ Level two	itch, titch, pitch, stitch, snitch, ditch, hitch, witch, switch, twitch, bitch, (rich, which)	skid, grid, slid, squid	sprig, twig, swig
brick, click, chick, trick, slick, stick, flick, thick, crick, prick, wick	still, spill, skill, drill, trill, frill, grill, swill, shrill, chill, thrill	skim, slim, brim, swim, whim, grim, prim, trim	chimp, limp, skimp, shrimp, scrimp,
spin, skin, grin, twin, thin, shin, chin,	ping, sting, king, bring, cling, sling, fling, wing, swing, zing, ring, spring, string, sing, thing,	ink, pink, stink, kink, rink, drink, mink, link, blink, clink, slink, wink, chink, brink, shrink, sink, think	hint, flint, glint, splint, mint, print, sprint, tint, stint, squint
snip, ship, skip, trip, flip, grip, clip, chip, whip, blip, slip, drip, strip,	bliss, Swiss, (this)	dish, fish, wish, Trish, swish, whish	disk, risk, brisk, frisk, whisk
crisp, wisp, lisp,	mist, list, fist, twist, whist,	spit, flit, grit, split, slit, twit	

Vowel Discrimination and Rimes List 2.

ă Level one	lab, dab, jab, cab, nab, tab,	pad, had, lad, fad, bad, mad, dad, sad,	rag, tag, sag, hag, bag, lag, wag, gag,
lack, rack, pack, sack, back, Jack,	jam, ham, Pam, ram, dam, Sam, yam	an, ban, Dan, pan, man, can, fan, ran, tan, van,	cap, lap, rap, map, gap, nap, sap, tap, yap
at, Pat, pat, sat, hat, cat, bat, rat, mat, fat, vat	mass, pass, lass,	Max, fax, tax	

ă Level two	flab, crab, grab, scab, blab, drab, slab, stab	clad, glad,	daft, raft, draft, graft, craft, shaft
brag, stag, snag, flag, drag, crag,	quack, flack, snack stack, crack, track, smack, black, slack, shack, whack,	slam, gram, dram, cram, pram, tram, sham, wham, swam, clam, glam,	champ, clamp, cramp, damp, lamp, ramp, scamp, stamp, tramp, camp
span, clan, plan, Stan, bran, Fran, flan, scan, Gran, than,	and, hand, sand, stand, band, land, grand, gland, brand	tang, pang, sang, hang, bang, rang, prang, clang, slang, fang, gang, twang, sprang	dank, hank, bank, rank, crank, drank, prank, yank, lank, tank, sank
blank, clank, plank, flank, Frank, thank	ant, chant, scant, pant, plant, slant, rant,	trap, slap, snap, clap, chap, flap, scrap, strap	brass, class, glass, grass,
stash, splash, dash, cash, bash, gash, rash, brash, crash, trash, mash, smash, clash, slash, flash,	cask, mask, flask, bask, task	clasp, grasp, gasp, rasp,	past, mast, cast, last, fast, blast, vast
spat, brat, flat, that, chat, scat, splat, slat, sprat, drat	patch, thatch, snatch, hatch, catch, batch, match, latch,	bath, path	blanch, ranch, branch

Vowel Discrimination and Rimes List 3.

ĕ Level one	Ted, Ned, bed, red, led, fed, zed	beg, peg, Meg, leg,	peck neck, deck,
tell, sell, dell, hell, bell, yell, fell, well, quell	ten, pen, hen, yen, Len, Den, den, Ken, Ben, men,	mess, less, Jess, Bess, Tess	let, get, jet, vet, wet net, set, pet, bet, yet, met,

ĕ Level two	sketch, retch, fetch, vetch, stretch,	Fred, shed, bled, fled, sled, sped, shred,	check, fleck, speck,
spell, smell, swell, shell, dwell	then, when, glen,	end, send, bend, mend, spend, lend, blend, trend,	tent, dent, spent, went, sent, bent, lent, Lent, vent, rent
cress, dress, press, bless, chess, stress,	pest, test, nest, best, west, vest, rest, jest, quest, best, crest, chest, zest	belt, felt, melt, pelt,	deft, left, cleft, theft,

ŏ Level one	job, hob, rob, mob, lob, Bob, fob, cob, Rob, sob,	cog, dog, bog, log, fog, jog, hog	sock, dock, rock mock, lock, Jock
top, hop, mop, lop, bop, cop, pop,	toss, boss, Ross, moss, loss,	pot, not hot, jot, cot, dot, rot, lot, got,	nod, pod, god, rod, cod,
box, fox,			

ŏ Level two	blob, slob, snob, throb,	notch, botch, blotch, splotch,	soft, loft, croft
smog, slog, flog, frog, clog	stock, smock, block, clock, frock, shock, flock, crock, stock	pond, frond, bond,	pong, song, prong, long, gong, strong, throng, thong
stop, crop, drop, prop, plop, slop, flop, shop, chop, strop	old, bold, cold, fold, gold, hold, sold, told	posh, dosh, cosh, gosh, Josh, slosh, tosh	spot, trot, blot, clot, plot, slot, swot, shot, Scot,
prod, trod, clod, plod, shod,	cross, floss, gloss, dross,	cost, lost, frost,	broth, moth, cloth, froth,

Vowel Discrimination and Rimes List 4.

ŭ Level one	tub, nub, sub, dub, hub, cub, rub, pub	bud, dud, mud, pud,	tug, pug, dug, hug, bug, rug, mug, lug, jug,
suck, duck, muck, luck, buck, ruck, tuck	pull, dull, hull, bull, full, gull, cull, lull, mull	sum, hum, mum, gum, bum, rum, yum	pun, nun, sun, bun, run, fun, gun,
up, cup, pup, sup,	put, nut, hut, cut, but, rut, gut, jut, tut		

ŭ Level two	stub, snub, grub, blub, club, scrub, shrub,	Dutch, hutch, butch, crutch, clutch, (such, much)	thud, scud, spud, stud,
snug, trug, smug, plug, slug, glug, shrug, chug, shrug, thug	stuck, truck, cluck, pluck, chuck, struck	buff, chuff, duff, puff, gruff, scruff, stuff	hunt, blunt, punt, runt, brunt, grunt, shunt, stunt,
chum, scum, glum, plum, slum, drum, scrum, strum, swum,	pump, stump, dump, hump, bump, rump, clump, plump, slump, thump, chump, jump, lump,	busk, dusk, husk, musk, rusk, tusk,	bunch, crunch, hunch, lunch, munch, punch, brunch, scrunch
		bust, dust, gust, just, lust, rust, crust, trust, thrust	
sung, stung, dung, hung, bung, rung, lung, clung, slung, flung, swung, sprung, strung,	punk, sunk, stunk, dunk, hunk, skunk bunk, drunk, trunk, clunk, slunk, flunk, junk, chunk,	push, hush, bush, lush, rush, mush, brush, crush, blush, plush, slush, flush, gush, thrush	dust, rust, crust, trust, must, just, gust, thrust
smut, glut, shut, strut	skull,	bulk, hulk, sulk	stun, spun, shun

Vowel Cross

This is a game for two or three players.

You will need:
1. A pencil
2. A blank piece of paper to keep score.
3. The 'Vowel Cross' paper.
4. One set of alphabet cards with the vowels taken out.

Before you begin:
1. Put the names of the players on the blank piece of paper. Leave room to write words under their names.
2. Write a vowel sound in the middle of each cross.
3. Mix up the alphabet cards and put them in a pile face down.

How to play:
1. The first player picks up an alphabet card.
2. Then writes that letter in a box on one of the vowel crosses.
3. The next player picks up a new card and does the same.
4. When players finish a word, they write it down on the score paper underneath their name.
5. The person with the most words at the end is the winner.

Rules:
1. Words can only be made from left to right and from top to bottom. They cannot be made to go backwards.
2. Each alphabet letter can only be used once.
3. You do not have to finish a vowel cross before starting another one.
4. You can choose not to write a letter down, but you cannot pick up another letter until it is your turn again.

Teacher Instructions on page 72.

Letter sound links

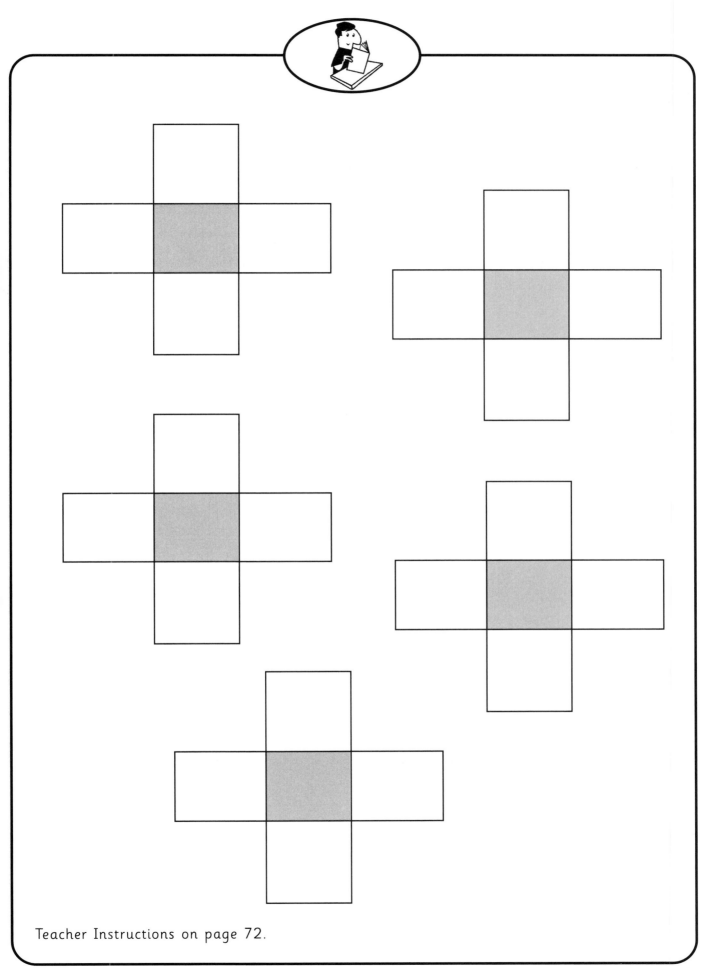

Teacher Instructions on page 72.

Top of the Tower

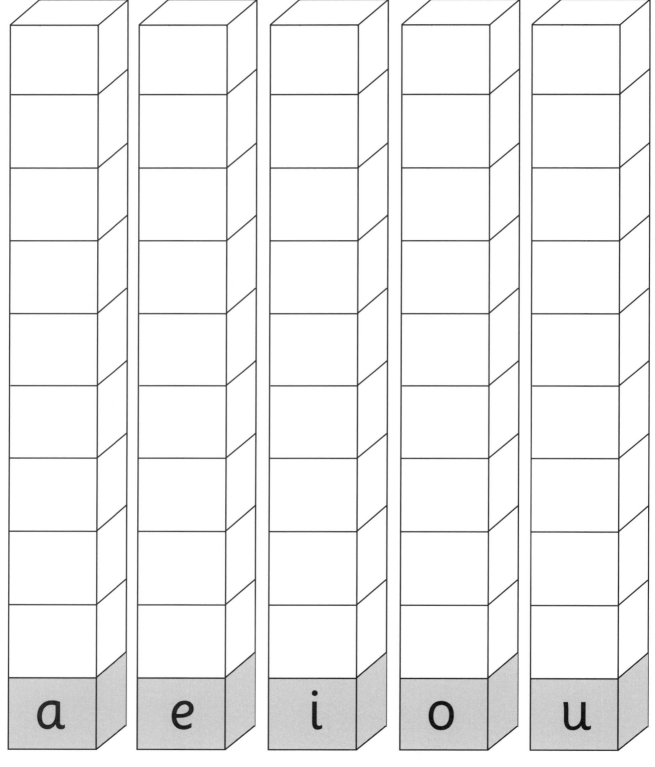

Teacher Instructions on Page 72.

Literacy homework

Name

Practise saying your memory pack: What to do

1. Hold the cards in your hand with the letter shapes looking at you.

2. Look at the top card but do not turn it over. Try to remember the picture on the back and say the word.

3. Then say the sound the word begins with. Now say the alphabet name of the letter.

4. Do it like this – 'tap', 'tuh', 'tee'. When you have said a card turn it over and check that you were right. If not do it again.

5. Say all the cards in your pack this way. Can you do them without help?

This work had:

☐ no help

☐ some help

☐ a lot of help

Parent signature/comment

Literacy homework

Name

Return by

Making words: What to do

1. Use the cards and sequencing board to make words.
   The white boxes on the board are for white cards.
   The blue boxes are for blue cards.

2. Can you make 6 words with your cards?
   The words should all have _____ in them.

3. Write the words down in a list.

4. Can you read the list?

This work had: **Parent signature/comment**

☐ no help

☐ some help

☐ a lot of help

Literacy homework

Name

Return by

Make a pairs game: What to do

1. Use the cards and sequencing board to make 5 words. The white boxes on the board are for white cards. The blue boxes are for blue cards. The words should all have _____ in them.

2. Cut a big piece of paper into 10 cards.

3. Write each word on 2 of the cards.

4. Now use them to play pairs with someone. Turn over all the cards and mix them up. Take it in turns to turn over 2 cards. Read each card. If the cards are the same, you can keep them. If not turn them back. The winner is the one with the most cards at the end. Don't forget to read the words!

This work had: **Parent signature/comment**

☐ no help

☐ some help

☐ a lot of help

Longer Words and Suffixes

The opportunity to read and spell longer words can be a tremendous boost to a learner's confidence. Working with phonically regular words of two syllables, compound words and simple suffixes is a way to do this without overburdening the learner with letter sound combinations for which they are not ready.

Syllables are the beats within words, each syllable contains a vowel. The word 'net' has one syllable, but the word 'magnet' has two, 'mag' and 'net'.

Compound words are words where each syllable is a short word in its own right, e.g. 'whiplash', 'hotpot', 'stopwatch'.

Suffixes are word endings that are added to a word base to change it into a new one, e.g. the past tense 'ed'.

Leading Activities

Two syllable words

Always work with two syllable words that follow the letter patterns of level one and level two; a useful list of these can be found on pages 92–3. You may need to practise some of the syllable activities on pages 14 and 15 first before working on some of the practical ideas in this section.

Dividing two syllable words

A simple technique can be used to show how to split two syllable words at level one and two into their separate beats. Such words, for example, 'magnet', 'plastic' and 'solvent' all have short vowel sounds within each syllable and contain a vccv pattern. The division technique is demonstrated below using the word 'magnet'.

Each vowel is marked with a 'v'. A 'c' is placed over the consonants in between the two vowels and a line drawn between them. The word is then split into its two syllables. Each syllable can now be read in turn and the syllables blended back together again to make a whole word.

$$\overset{\text{v \quad c \quad c \quad v}}{\text{magnet}}$$

$$\text{m ag} | \text{net}$$

This technique is useful for choosing appropriate words for the learner to work with and to teach as a reading skill for attacking unfamiliar words. Remember to use a multi-sensory approach wherever possible and to practise both blending and segmenting syllables.

Longer words and suffixes

Compound Words

whip	lash

The same division technique can be used with compound words as with other two syllable words. Learners are often surprised to see two little words they know put together to make a longer one that they thought they didn't!

Adding Suffixes

Learning how to work with suffixes can make a big impact on spelling and on reading accuracy. The key to this is being able to identify the base first and then knowing how the suffix is added. Learners therefore need to practise reading and spelling word bases with and without their suffixes.

word base   suffix   new word

stand + ing   = standing

Sometimes the suffix can just be added to the base without making any changes; sometimes the word has to be changed first, for example, doubling the 'n' in 'run' to make 'running' (see page 102).

In this set of resources, three basic suffixes are used:

Plural 's' and 'es' – which means 'more than one' e.g. bat**s**, cap**s**, tin**s**, glass**es**, box**es**

Suffix 'ing' – which is added to a verb or doing word and shows the present tense, e.g. nodd**ing**, stopp**ing**, robb**ing**

Suffix 'ed' – which is also added to a verb and shows the past tense, e.g. nodd**ed**, push**ed**, robb**ed**. As you say these three words listen to the three different pronunciations, /ed/ /t/ and /d/. The first one is the least common.

When beginning to work with suffixes, it is best to use base words that will not need to change when the suffix is added. Move on to changing the base word once this has been accomplished.

Two-syllable and Compound Words

Using Picture Clues, page 91

Using the pictures on page 91 or magazine pictures of words with two syllables, practise saying the words and emphasising their two beats. Clapping, tapping or nodding at the same time may help. The pictures can also be cut into two pieces and moved apart as the words are spoken to visually represent segmenting the two syllables. Conversely, the two parts of the picture can be moved together to represent blending the syllables to build a word. The words on page 91 are tennis, basket, chicken, rabbit, cricket, tandem, helmet, blanket, traffic, padlock, puppet, cactus.

Syllable partners

Working in pairs for the above activities can be fun. The first person says the first syllable and then the second person completes the word by saying the second syllable. The partners can then swap over.

Building Two-syllable Words with Sequencing Boards and Memory Packs

Regular two-syllable words which contain a vccv pattern can be built using a learner's memory pack (page 58) and the use of two sequencing boards (see page 66) that are placed end to end.

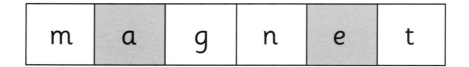

| m | a | g | n | e | t |

Two-syllable Word and Sentence List

A list of useful two syllable words linked to the letter sound order of the memory packs is given on pages 92–3. Use this to structure the introduction of longer words. The list also includes example sentences for reading and dictation.

Compound Jig Words page 94

Use the set of single words to combine together to make longer compound words. This can be an individual activity or the words can be made into cards and played as 'Pairs'. Each player turns over two cards. If they can be combined to make a longer word, the player keeps them. If not the cards are turned over again. The player with the most cards at the end is the winner.

See also the homework activities on pages 95–7

Pictures for Two-syllable Words

Teacher Instructions on page 90.

Word and Sentence List

The following list of words and sentences are given in the order that the letter sounds occur in the chart on page 56–7. In this way if the learners are ready, they can be introduced to longer words as they work through the programme. Working with two-syllable words can be accomplished at level one without the use of letter blends and digraphs, but is probably best tackled with those who are working at level two.

a	pasta
	Pat's pasta is in a pan.
d	distant
	Stan's dad is sad and distant.
h	hatpin, hidden
	Sid has hidden a hatpin in his hand.
e	dentist, tennis, happen, pendant, snippet, Tessa, Dennis, tenpin
	Dennis sent Tessa a pendant.
c	picnic, cancan
	Dennis and his dad sat in the sand and had a picnic.
k	kidnap, ticket, kitten, catkin, kennel, packet, napkin, sicken, picket
	Ken's pet kitten taps at the catkin.
b	bandit, basket, disband
	The bandit spat in the sand.
r	rabbit, racket, ransack
	The best trick is the rabbit in the hat.
br	bracken, bracket, Brenda
	Brenda kicks the tennis racket and bends it.
cr	crimson, cricket
	Tessa's best dress is crimson red.
dr	drastic
	It's a bit drastic!
tr	trespass, triplet, Tristan
	Rick, Stan and Tristan are triplets.
m	Batman, misfit, dismiss, tandem, mitten, damsel, mishap, madcap, miscast, muffin
	Batman kisses the damsel in distress.
y	Yasmin
	Yasmin has a mishap and dents the tandem.
l	tinsel, helmet, tassel, Scotland, pellet, silken, rascal, sandal, signal, tablet, Lisbet
	Miss Scotland's sandals have silken tassels.
bl	blanket
	The tramp sits in his blanket and has a rest.
cl	classic
	Mick mends the dent in the back of the classic tram.
pl	plastic, plimsoll
	Are all Kit-Kats in a red plastic packet?

Longer words and suffixes

sl	slacken **The tent slackens in the damp.**
f	traffic, fitment, Finland, fitness, stiffen, midriff, fillet, sinful, misfit **Is Lisbet still in Finland?**
fl	flannel, flatten **The fat cat sits on the plant and flattens it.**
fr	Fredrick **Fredrick had a mint at the red traffic signal.**
o	padlock, tiptop, cannot, fossil, petrol, compass, socket, rotten, pollen, pocket, pistol, lesson, hammock, combat, bonnet, problem, locket, contest, spotless **He did not trespass and the compass and map led him back to the camp.**
g	golden, maggot, goblin, goblet, gallop, gossip, piglet, pigment, gimmick, goddess **The goddess had a sip of milk from a golden goblet.**
gl	glisten, glasses, glutton, Glennis **Glennis is glad she has got glasses.**
u	rustic, nugget, suspect, success, suspend, sudden, puppet, submit, summit, Muslim, hiccup, discuss, cactus, bullet, button, trumpet, tunnel, funnel, bucket **The bullets from the suspect's pistol are still in his pocket.**
j	jacket, subject, flapjack **Mrs Jennet's flapjack is the best in the contest and she must get the cup.**
v	velvet, vessel, victim, vandal, solvent, Melvin, Kelvin, Elvis, Denzil **All the Elvis fans had velvet jackets with golden buttons.**
w	cobweb, wigwam, nitwit, wicked, wicket, wilful, wisdom, witness, wombat **The wicked goblin sticks his victims to a vast cobweb.**
tw	twinset, twiglet **Kelvin is wilful and snacks on Twiglets, nuts and crisps.**
x	context, complex, convex, suffix **It is a complex problem that I cannot fix.**
z	zigzag **The witness told him that the van had skidded in a zigzag across the bend.**
qu	conquest, banquet, quintet, quicken, quilted **The jazz quintet got a hundred quid at the banquet.**
th	thicken, thicket, thinnest, Sabbath, Kenneth **Kenneth rests in his hammock on the Sabbath.**
sh	skittish, selfish, catfish, flatfish, bulrush, rubbish **The path was spotless until the vandals put rubbish on it.**
ch	chaffinch, channel, chicken, mismatch, dispatch **The traffic went in the Channel tunnel inch by inch.**
wh	whizzing **It was such a shock when the jets went whizzing past!**
ng	gosling, stocking, stuffing, swelling, wedding, decking **The best man kept the wedding ring in his pocket.**

Compound Words

Can you put two short words together to make longer words?

dish	top	fish	sun
chop	bull	sticks	dog
hand	shot	snap	cuffs
wind	bin	cloth	desk
shell	set	mill	dust

Literacy homework

Name	Return by

Joining two syllables to make longer words: What to do

Syllables are the beats in words.
'Egg' has one beat. 'Pudding' has two – 'pud' and 'ding'.
Can you put these syllables together to make a shopping list? Write down the list.

First syllable

len flap had muf pas

chip scam chic pud pump

Second syllable

dock kin sticks ding tils

jack ken fins ta pi

This work had:

☐ no help

☐ some help

☐ a lot of help

Parent signature/comment

Literacy homework

Name

Return by

Splitting words into two syllables: What to do

Syllables are the beats in words. Bath has one syllable. London has two.

1. Can you split these place names into two beats?

2. See if you can find the places in an atlas.

Bristol Penrith Swindon Bodmin Bexhill

Chigwell Rutland Boston Matlock Skegness

Cumnock Kinross

This work had:

Parent signature/comment

☐ no help

☐ some help

☐ a lot of help

Literacy homework

Name

Return by

Making compound words: What to do

Compound words are words that are made up of two smaller words joined together.

1. Can you add a word from the list below to the end of each of these to make a longer word?

2. Can you think of any more words you could put with sun?

Gold_ _ _ _   Sun_ _ _   Quick_ _ _ _

bath_ _ _   dust_ _ _   Bull_ _ _   hang_ _ _

Bat_ _ _   man_ _ _ _   dish_ _ _ _ _

(man   set   cloth   tub   dog   fish   sand
man   trap   bin)

This work had: **Parent signature/comment**

☐ no help

☐ some help

☐ a lot of help

Plural 's' and 'es'

Plural 's'

Adding plural 's' to words that end with a short vowel sound followed by a single consonant or consonant blend, e.g. '**tin**' **tins**, '**st_ep_** st**eps**', and '**b_end_** b**ends**' is straight forward. These word patterns just involve adding the 's' which the learner needs to know means 'more than one'.

The plural can therefore be added to words throughout the teaching programme, during word building, reading and in sentence dictation once the letter 's' has been taught. Scan texts that have been read in shared reading for the plural or make it the focus of a guided reading activity.

Discuss the way the 's' sounds like 'z' at the ends of some words, e.g. 'tins'.

At this stage avoid words that end in 'f' 'y' 'ch' 'sh' 'ss' 'x' or with a vowel, as they involve more complicated manoeuvres such as adding 'es' or 'ies' or 'ves'.

Avoid also teaching possessive 's' until plural 's' is secure. Many adults mix up the two as in the greengrocer's sign- 'Plum's twenty pence a pound'.

Just add plural 's' page 99

Use this activity sheet to reinforce the word building you have been working on.

Plural 'es' page 100

When a word ends with 'ss' 'x' 'ch/tch' or 'sh' the plural 'es' is added. This also adds another syllable to the word, e.g. glass becomes 'glasses' or box becomes 'boxes'.

Choose words that have this pattern from the list on page 100. Use them in word building and word reading activities.

Hot and Cold Snacks page 101

This activity has mixed 's' and 'es'. Encourage the readers to keep asking themselves 'Is there more than one?'

See also the homework activities on page 113

Just Add Plural 's'

Add plural 's' to these words.
Write the new word next to the old one.
Can you read the words?

cat _____   step _____   sock _____

tin _____   flag _____   disk _____

hat _____   spot _____   bill _____

tap _____   frog _____   bump _____

bag _____   duck _____   plant _____

pen _____   test _____   swing_____

Now write a sentence for each picture

_____

_____

Plural 'es'

Plural means more than one.

To add the plural to words
that end in 'ss' 'ch' 'sh' or 'x'
you have to use 'es'.

Which words need 'es'? Underline them.

class, pen, crash, match, twig, fox, crutch, cross, bunch, bag, sketch, brush, blotch, chip, dress, box, glass, shop, splash, patch, hutch, lunch, bush, punch

Can you finish these sentences ?

1. Rabbits live in _____.

2. Ripped things are fixed with _____.

3. Children at school are put in _____.

4. Fresh eggs are sold in _____.

5. Old lamps are lit with _____.

6. Milk is drunk from _____.

7. Packed lunches are put in _____.

8. Rubbish is swept up with _____.

9. A red rash has lots of _____.

Mixed 's' and 'es'

Hot and Cold Snacks

Linda runs a snack van at the truck stop. She got in such a rush that she missed off the plurals from these order slips. Can you put them in?

---

2 bag of chip
2 can of pop

---

3 hot cross bun
   and a pot of jam
3 mug of coffee

---

4 jacket spud with
   salad
4 glass of milk

---

1 ham sandwich
2 egg sandwich
1 pot of tea for 3

---

2 packet of crisp
1 can of pop
1 glass of lemon crush

---

2 nut cutlet
2 french stick
2 cup of tea

---

4 rock bun
1 jug of still lemon and
4 glass

---

1 scotch egg and chip
2 lentil hotpot
3 lemon crush

---

1 bag of crisp
1 bag of nut
2 cup of tea

---

3 chicken nugget
3 hot chilli dip
3 can of pop

Present tense 'ing'

Suffix 'ing'

This suffix is added to verbs to show the present tense.

Just add 'ing'

Initially choose verbs that end in two consonants, such as 'pack,' 'send' and 'fill' or words that end in 'x' such as 'fax'. These word patterns only require the 'ing' to be added on the end with no doubling. Use the list of words on pages 76–9 to help you.

As suffix 'ing' has the 'ng' sound at the end of it, it may best to wait until that sound has been covered in a learner's programme. By that point, a learner's memory pack has sufficient cards in it to build a range of 'doing words'.

Alternatively the 'ing' can be taught as a rime without addressing the 'ng' sound and can be added much earlier. Remember to stick to words that are made up of the sounds within the learner's pack.

Double and 'ing'

Words that end in a short vowel sound followed by a single consonant, need to have their final consonant doubled before adding 'ing'. The rule the learner needs to learn is that there should be two consonants before the 'ing'. If there are two consonants already, just add 'ing', if not double and add 'ing'. The exception to this is 'x' where the two phonemes /ks/ are represented by one letter.

Fling on the 'ing', Double then add 'ing' and 'The Camping Trip pages 103–5

Use these activity sheets to structure the introduction of 'ing' from no doubling, to doubling, to mixed sets of words

See also the homework activities on page 114

Just Add 'ing'

Fling on the 'ing'

| ing | fl i**ng** | fl i**ng**ing |

1. Mark the vowel in each word below.

2. Highlight all the consonants that come after each vowel.

3. How many consonants are there at the end of each word?

4. When there are two consonants at the end, just add 'ing'.

5. Now add 'ing' to each word and write down the new word you have made.

j u m p   jumping   stand _____

lift   _____   pull   _____

push   _____   bend   _____

spring   _____   rush   _____

land   _____   fling   _____

twist   _____   catch   _____

Double Then Add 'ing'

Double and Fling

ing

p u t

p u**tt**in g

1. Mark the vowel in each word below.

2. Highlight all the consonants that come after each vowel.

3. How many consonants are there at the end of each word?

4. When there is just one consonant at the end, you need to double the consonant and then add 'ing'.

5. Now add 'ing' to each word and write down the new word you have made.

h ⓘ t	hitting	grip	_____
win	_____	skip	_____
hop	_____	run	_____
swim	_____	step	_____
sit	_____	trip	_____
jog	_____	spin	

Adding 'ing' – The Camping Trip

 Remember: Two consonants – just add 'ing'. One consonant – double then add 'ing'

Add 'ing' and fill in the gaps

think	camp	pitch	club	wish
clap	sip	shop	thrill	spend
grab	rest	chat	sing	tan

Dear Pat,

Our _____ trip went well. _____ our

tent was a bit stressful, but we did it in the end. Then we

sat on the sun beds _____ and _____

ourselves. Lunch was spent by the pool _____

and _____ cold drinks. We went _____

until we dropped, _____ too much cash. And after

_____ a quick snack, we went _____.

Everyone was _____ and _____ to the

band. It was _____! We couldn't help

_____ we didn't have to go back.

_____ of you, Sam. xx

Past Tense 'ed'

Suffix 'ed' is added to verbs to indicate the past tense.

Understanding 'verb' and 'past tense'

If learners are unsure of the term 'verb' try sorting 'doing words' from a set of pictures that illustrate both nouns and verbs. Creating a mime for each one adds extra interest.

It may also be necessary to explain the meaning of the 'past' through sequencing pictures that show actions that are about to happen, ones that are in progress and actions that have finished. These might include a picture of someone about to jump, someone jumping in the air and someone who has already jumped and landed. Link these pictures to the spoken words 'going to jump', 'jumping' and 'jumped'.

Video footage of sporting events can also be useful; use the pause button and move the video on frame by frame and create your own commentary for an action replay.

Recognising suffix 'ed'

Using sets of pictures as above, match a word card, such as 'jumped', to the correct illustration. Underline the 'ed' ending. Highlight 'ed' endings within sentences and texts.

Adding 'ed'

Suffix 'ed' is added to words in the same way as 'ing'. The same rule about doubling consonants applies (see page 102). Use the word lists on page 76–9 to choose words with which to work. Make the words out of letter cards or write them on mini-whiteboards. Work with base words that do not require changing first; move on to doubling afterwards. Present tense words such as 'blend<u>s</u>' and 'spill<u>s</u>' require the 's' to be before adding 'ed'.

Manipulating 'ed'

Include plenty of practice in manipulating base words and their endings through both adding 'ed' and taking it away.

Just Add 'ed' and Double and 'ed' pages 109–10.

Use these two activity sheets as independent revision of the skills you have taught.

Appreciating the different sounds suffix 'ed' makes

Suffix 'ed' has three different sounds /t/ /d/ and /ed/. The last one is the least common and applies to base words ending with the sound /t/ or /d/ such as 'do**t**' or 'men**d**' giving the words 'dotted' and 'mended'. Suffix 'ed' sounds like /t/ when it is added

to verbs that end with unvoiced sounds such as /k/ /f/ /p/ /s/ /x/ as in 'pic**k**ed', 'snif**f**ed', 'ho**p**ped' 'pas**s**ed' and 'fi**x**ed'. But it sounds like /d/ when added to voiced sounds such as the vowels and /b/ /g/ /l/ /m/ n/ /v/ /z/ as in 'st**ay**ed', 'ro**b**bed', 'be**g**ged', 'fil**l**ed', 'sla**m**med', 'sa**v**ed', and 'fi**z**zed'. **For most of the learners you work with, these 'rules' will be too complex;** they are listed here for teacher interest only. Instead, work on listening to and appreciating the different pronunciations and agreeing which ones 'sound' right. Learners can hold up cards representing the different sounds that suffix 'ed' makes.

'ed' Dominoes page 108

This is a game, for two to four players, which helps discriminate between the different sounds that 'ed' makes. Share the dominoes equally between the players. During the game the two types of domino must be placed on the table alternately. For example, if the first player lays down the domino 'fizzed/dusted' the next player has to put down either a domino with 'sounds like /d/' in front of 'fizzed' or one that has 'sounds like /ed/' after 'dusted'. The winner is the first person to play all their dominoes.

Shared reading – Super Ed page 111

This text can be used as a shared or independent reading activity. When the text has been read, scan the text again for all the action/doing words. Not all are 'ed' words; there are a few examples of irregular verbs too. Use a highlighter pen to mark all the 'ed' words. Listen to the different sounds that the 'ed' ending makes. Ask the reader to identify the base word for each 'ed' word. There are examples of 'just add' and 'double'.

Writing – Robbery at Milton Cross page 112

Use this story idea as a basis for creative writing where the writer has to remember how to apply the 'ed' ending. The instructions contain a number of 'ed' words that will serve as a reminder to 'just add' and 'double'. Ask the writer to watch out for all the verbs they use. Some further useful words are included at the end to help the story flow.

Irregular verbs

There are a number of irregular forms of the past tense that do not use the suffix 'ed', e.g. we say 'ran' not 'runned' and 'caught' not 'catched'. In the same way that young children over apply the past tense when learning to speak, you may find that your developing spellers do the same. When this occurs ask them to say the word within a sentence and to listen if it sounds right. More often than not they will be able to hear the error for themselves. The irregular forms are best learned as exceptions to the rule as they occur. They can be learned as individual sight words or along with other words with the same rime pattern at the end.

See also the homework activities on page 115

'ed' dominoes

Teacher Instructions on page 107. (Cut along the dotted lines only)

picked	filled	sounds like /d/	sounds like /ed/
begged	skidded	sounds like /ed/	sounds like /t/
filled	dusted	sounds like /ed/	sounds like /t/
hopped	robbed	sounds like /d/	sounds like /t/
jumped	added	sounds like /ed/	sounds like /d/
twisted	sniffed	sounds like /t/	sounds like /t/

Just Add 'ed'

Can you underline the doing words?

1. The last man checks the lock.

2. Mick blends the eggs and the milk.

3. The duck quacks at the fox.

4. Pat spills his drink on the rug.

5. Tessa bumps into Jill at the fish shop.

6. Stan plants them in the pumpkin patch.

7. Sam tricks his chums and gets the last chip.

Take off the 's' to find the base words. Now change them into the past tense.

Can you take off suffix 'ed' and find the base word?

1. splashed _____

2. itched _____

3. acted _____

4. licked _____

5. twisted _____

6. camped _____

7. blocked _____

Double and 'ed'

Change these words into the past tense.

grin   _____

skid   _____

fit   _____

shop   _____

drip   _____

tan   _____

drop   _____

sip   _____

Now put the words into these sentences.

1. Tom _____ at his cold drink.

2. Dennis _____ at Ben.

3. The tap _____ into the sink.

4. The bus _____ into the van.

5. The red dress _____ well.

6. His back was _____ from the sun.

7. Kim and Fran _____ 'til they _____.

Reading 'ed' – Super Ed

Super Ed is an all action hero.

- Underline the action words in this newspaper story about him.
- Make a list of all the base words that have had 'ed' added to them

MASKED MAN HAS A LOT OF BOTTLE

At six a.m. last Monday, milkman Bill Smith kicked himself on the shin when he ran out of petrol. His milk van bumped to a stop on the bend just by the flats at Milton Cross. Milk bottles clinked and clanked as traffic rushed by and rocked the van.

In an exclusive report for the Sunday Blast, Bill told us how he jumped out just as a bus whizzed past and a stack of milk fell from the back. The bottles smashed into bits and glass shot everywhere. Milk splashed across the road.

Bill told us he scanned up and down and called for help and then jumped out of his skin when he felt a sudden tap on the back.

When he checked what it was, he was shocked to find that it was a man in a mask. Bill was thrilled when the masked man, known as Super Ed, pushed the milk van off the road and brushed up the glass before he rushed off to save the planet.

Bill Smith told the Daily Blast that the masked man had felt sad about the mess that was left and had wanted to mop up the milk. "I told him not to bother about that," bragged a very flushed Bill. "I mean, it's no good crying over spilt milk, is it?"

Writing 'ed' – Robbery at Milton Cross

ed

The Bank at Milton Cross was robbed last month. The robber pinched sixty thousand pounds. The police looked everywhere but could not find the culprit or the cash.

The police called in Super Ed. The all action hero helped them catch the robber and found where the cash had been stashed.

Can you write the newspaper report for the Sunday Blast telling how Super Ed used his super-human skills to save the day?

Remember to use the 'ed' ending to put the story in the past tense.

Useful words

footprint	money	stole	chased
getaway	loot	car	flew
clue	alarm	safe	hideaway
took	found	behind	reward
road	sound	caught	said
robber	police	hero	dangerous

Literacy homework

Name

Return by

Plural means more than one : What to do

1. Underline the right plural in the bracket.

tin (tins tines)   push (pushs pushes)   step (steps stepes)

wish (wish wishes) crisp (crisps crispes)   tick (ticks tickes)

box (box boxes)   match (matchs matches) kiss (kiss kisses)

2. Write the plural for these words.

dish _____   bag _____   fox _____

This work had: **Parent signature/comment**

☐ no help

☐ some help

☐ a lot of help

Literacy homework

Name

Return by

Adding 'ing': What to do

1. Add 'ing' to these words.

2. Remember, if there are two consonants at the end – just add 'ing'.

3. If there is only one, double the consonant and then add 'ing'.

drip	plan	send	ring	sell	nod
quit	rip	act	get	shop	mend
hug	wish	fill	cut	jump	hit

This work had: **Parent signature/comment**

☐ no help

☐ some help

☐ a lot of help

Literacy homework

Name

Return by

Past tense 'ed' : What to do

You will need: The sports page from a newspaper.

1. Find ten words that have the past tense 'ed' at the end.

2. Write down each word and then write the base word next to it. Write them like this.

1. jumped   jump   2. ended   end

This work had: **Parent signature/comment**

☐ no help

☐ some help

☐ a lot of help

Irregular Words and Homophones

Irregular words and homophones

Irregular words do not follow a regular phonic pattern and are difficult to decode. They need a visual and kinaesthetic approach to enable them to be recognised by sight. Complex words that are regular but are too difficult for a beginner reader to analyse can be treated in the same way.

Function Words are the every day words that bind sentences together, for example, the words 'are', 'there', 'to' and 'said'.

Homophones are words that sound the same such as 'their' and 'there', but look different. They also benefit from visual and kinaesthetic techniques to enable the learner to distinguish between them.

Sight words are so familiar to readers that they can recognise them without having to do any conscious letter sound analysis. Recognising words by sight speeds up the reading process, allowing the reader to concentrate on meaning not decoding.

An Initial Sight Vocabulary is a store of sight words which has been built up before letter sound correspondence has been learned and is important stage for beginner readers. It is through these first words that they understand the symbolic nature of print and can begin to understand the difference between words and letters.

Visual Learners There are always some learners within a class whose preferred learning style is visual. The activities suggested in this section allow such learners to use these strengths to acquire new words. Visual analogies with other words that follow a similar letter sound pattern can then be made.

Which Words? The words that tend to be the most easily learned at an early stage are ones that are highly motivating or are able to be visualised pictorially by the learner, e.g. family or pop stars' names or common nouns. It is always interesting to see young readers recognising the long names of their favourite television programme or restaurant chain yet struggling with a shorter word such as 'said'.

The harder words to learn are the function words that do not have an easy visual image. But although they are harder to learn they are essential if the reader is to combine their store of sight words into sentences.

The National Literacy Strategy has lists of high and medium frequency words that are important for beginner readers to know as they occur so frequently in written language. But note how many of the 'hard to learn' function words are in these lists.

A Visual Kinaesthetic Approach

Use the activities in this section to build up sight words for beginners, to learn irregular or 'tricky' words or to distinguish between homophones for more advanced learners.

Introducing a New Word

New words should arise from a meaningful context to support understanding. The word should first be experienced as part of a sentence, the more memorable the better. With a younger child this might come from a favourite story or with an older learner it could be linked to a magazine article or internet page. The sentence can be read alongside the teacher, with the learner being encouraged to point to the words as they are read. The target word can then be highlighted and isolated from the other words, perhaps by drawing a line underneath it or writing it on a mini white board.

Link the Word to Real Objects, Pictures or Symbols

If the word to be learned is a noun it can be written on card and matched to a real object or to a picture, helping to create a visual image of the object it represents. If the word is a function word it may be possible to link it to a picture symbol or rebus such as those in 'Writing with Symbols', 'Mayer Johnson', or 'Clicker'. For readers with significant difficulties in learning, new words may need to be presented alongside pictures or symbols for some time. If this is so try gradually reducing the size of the picture so the written word becomes more prominent before fading it out altogether.

Teach 'How to Study a Word' and Use a Word Learning Routine

When we ask a learner to 'look' at a word, in order to learn it, we need to show them how to study it carefully, looking and talking about its salient features. (See page 121).

Then teach the learning routine on page 122, so they can become more independent in acquiring new words.

Practise Selecting the New Word from a Group

Once a new word has been introduced it should then be included within a group of words. The reader should then practise discriminating between these words to find the new one. With beginner readers this can be done in two different ways:

Word to Picture

1. The learner looks at the target word and matches it to the correct picture from a set of four pictures. The target word is then read.

Irregular words and homophones

Picture to Word

2. The learner looks at the target picture and matches it to the correct word within a set of four words. The target word is then read.

Practise Using the New Word within Sentences

Provide sentences that contain the new word on strips of card for the reader to practise reading. Once the sentence has been read it can be cut into individual words and shuffled to be reassembled by the learner. The new word can be incorporated into card word banks, or into word grids in a computer programme such as 'Clicker', where it can be used to create new sentences.

Matching Sentences to Pictures

Use sets of pictures and sentences that differ only slightly from each other to ensure the reader really understands what has been read. For example, a mixed set of pictures and sentences that represent 'The cat is sitting in a box.' 'The dog is sitting in a box.' 'The cat is sitting on a box.' and 'The dog is sitting under a box.'

Make Personalised Books

Sentences can be illustrated either through the learner's own drawings, magazine cuttings, clipart or photographs and made into personalised books. A computer programme such as 'Clicker' enables books to be made very easily and professionally. These can even incorporate scanned images, video material and sound to make the book a multi media one. The 'Clicker' programme also includes the facility for the computer to read the text or unfamiliar words to the reader.

Use the New Words within Games

Word games such as Lotto, Dominoes, Pairs and Snap are traditionally used as early sight vocabulary activities. Board games can also easily be adapted to include reading target words. Older learners might like to design their own games that incorporate new words within a theme that interests them, such as football or bird watching.

A Teaching Order for NLS High Frequency and Medium Frequency Words

The check list on pages 56–7 includes NLS high and medium frequency words and a suggested order for teaching these within the step-by-step letter sound programme.

The teaching order relates to the letter sounds that have been learned, thus having learned the letters 'itpnsad' the learner is introduced to the irregular word 'said' to learn by sight. As 'said' is made up of only letters that have been covered

so far, the learner will be familiar with the visual appearance of the letters and their names in order to study the word efficiently.

Use the assessment on pages 166–7 to identify which High frequency words are already known. Highlight the ones still to be learned on the letter sound checklist and include work on these as you progress through the programme. Once sight words are known they can be included within sentence dictation and sentence reading activities.

Studying a Word

Many learners when asked to 'look at a word' in order to learn it do not know where to begin. They may glance at it, perhaps taking in its first few letters but do not study the word in a systematic way noting any salient features that will make it memorable.

The following teaching techniques should be used when a new irregular word is introduced. They should be used in conjunction with the learning routine on page 122.

Talk about the Word and highlight any interesting features when they are noticed.

- **Look at the individual letters within a word.** What letter does the word begin with? Which is the last letter? Is the word a long or a short word? How many letters does it have? Do you know the names of all the letters in the word?
- **Are there any letters that are in the word more than once?** Draw attention to words that begin and end with the same letter. Perhaps there is a double letter to note, like the 'ee' in 'green' or the 'tt' in 'little'.
- **Does the word remind you of one you already know?** Perhaps it has the same letters in it that are in the learner's name, or the name of the school.
- **Does the word share the same rime with another word?** An analogy can then be drawn, for example knowing the word 'house' can help with 'mouse'.
- Are there any hidden words within the word? For example, 'woman' has 'man' at the end; the word 'also' has 'so' at the end, 'London' has two 'ons' in it.
- **Is there anything odd about the word?** Perhaps it has a silent letter, or a 'c' that is 'soft' and pronounced like an 's'.

Play the missing letter game

After studying a word and highlighting the salient features, write it on a white board asking the learner to look at it closely again and recall the letter sequence. Then ask them to close their eyes while you rub out part of the word. You may erase a single letter or a group of letters; this will depend on the features you have discussed. Can the learner say what is missing and write it in? Do this several times with different features of the word. Then rub out the whole word and ask the learner to write it independently.

See also the homework activities on page 124–5

Word Learning Routine

Many reading schemes include the 'look-cover-write-check' approach to learning a new word. The multi-sensory approach used here combines this with the 'SOS' (Simultaneous Oral Spelling) of Bryant and Bradley (1985) and Hickey (Combley 2001). Note that the approach uses letter names and not letter sounds, as it is a technique for learning irregular words or for those learners who find letter – sound correspondence difficult.

Teach the following word learning routine and give the learner a copy of the prompt sheet on page 123.

- **Look at the word** and study its salient features (see page 121).
- **Say the word** listening carefully to it as it is spoken.
- **Name the letters** in sequence, first when looking at the word then with eyes closed.
- **Trace over the letters** with a finger or a pencil to feel the shape of the word and the letters within it, saying the names of the letters as they are traced.
- **Copy the word** underneath or on another piece of paper, saying the letter names.
- **Hide the word** and try to 'see' it in your mind.
- **Write the word from memory** naming the letters as you do so. Hickey's method also follows this with writing the word with the eyes shut.
- **Check the word** to see if it is correct; if not identify the mistake and correct it.
- **Repeat** the learning routine for each new word three times.

Once the learner has done this it should be used and checked frequently within their learning sessions to ensure that it is mastered. Include the word in sentence dictation, look for it during reading sessions and incorporate it into word games.

See also the homework activities on page 124–5

Learning a New Word

	Look at the word
	Say the word
	Name the letters
	Trace the letters
	Hide the word
	Write the word and name the letters 
	Check the word

Literacy homework

Name

Return by

Learning New Words: What to do

1. Can you learn to read and spell these words?

_____   _____   _____

_____   _____   _____

_____   _____   _____

Use the sheet 'Learning a New Word' to help you.
Practise each word three times then have a break.

2. After a few minutes try and remember the words again.

Practise each word again three times.

3. Can you still remember them in the morning?

This work had: **Parent signature/comment**

☐ no help

☐ some help

☐ a lot of help

Literacy homework

Name

Return by

Learning a Tricky word: What to do

The tricky word is _____.

The first letter is _____.

The last letter is _____.

It has the letter _____ in the middle.

There are _____ letters altogether.

Try to notice something special about the word to help you.

The special thing is

_____

_____

_____

Now use the sheet 'Learning a New Word' to help you remember the word.

This work had: Parent signature/comment

☐ no help

☐ some help

☐ a lot of help

Common 'th' words

The following words beginning with 'th' frequently cause learners difficulty. Some of them can be decoded phonically but it may be useful to work on them visually as a whole set when the letter sound 'th' is introduced.

First check which ones the learner already knows.

the	**th**is	**th**at	**th**ere	**th**an	**th**ey	**th**eir
then	**th**em	**th**ese	wi**th**			

These number words are useful to teach together

three	**th**irteen	**th**irty

The Activity sheet 'West Cliff' on page 128 can be used to reinforce the 'th' words

Homophones: Their or there?

Sometimes these two words become a real stumbling block for learners. The word 'their' always means 'belonging to them'. The word 'there' is used to indicate a place or in the phrase 'there is' or 'there are'. Use the following symbols to help illustrate the difference in meaning.

See also the homework activities on page 135

Activity Sheet 'Their or There' on page 127 can be used once the difference between the two homophones is understood.

Their or There? – Pat and Tom's shopping

Can you fill in the missing words?

Pat and Tom had **their** shopping list...

their

there

..and went to the shop over **there**.

Pat and Tom went to do _____ shopping. "Go and get a trolley," said Pat. Tom went to hunt for one at the back of the shop. "No silly!" shouted Pat pointing to the tills at the front. "You get them _____!"

Tom found one and pushed it back to Pat. They began to do _____ shopping. But Tom kept pushing the trolley too fast and _____ shopping fell out. Pat picked up _____ things. "Watch what you're doing," she snapped. "I think I'll do the pushing, you go and get the milk from over _____."

Just then, Pat saw her friend Debra. "Cooeee! Debs!" she called, letting go of the trolley. "Oh no, look out!" she yelled, as it crashed into some tins. A shop assistant rushed over to Pat and yelled, "Just look what you have done over _____!" She pushed past Pat and went over to the tins to stack them up again. "Yes, "said Tom, coming back with the milk. " Why don't you look where you're going?"

Pat and Tom put the rest of _____ things in _____ trolley and took it to the checkout. When they got back to _____ car, Tom looked at Pat. She was very red and flushed. "It was hot in _____ wasn't it?" she said. "I don't know how the people that work in _____ keep _____ cool!"

Common 'th' Words – 'West Cliff'

1. Can you find these 'th' words in the story? Highlight or underline them.

there	three	thin	thrill	other	brothers
this	together	thirty	these	thought	this
they	the	that	path	through	earth
than	their	them	then	with	

There were once three brothers, Stan, Fred and Jack. Stan was tall, but Fred was the tallest. Jack was small and thin.

The three brothers got on well with each other. They were the best of pals. They had to be, for they had lived together at 'West Cliff' for thirty years.

'West Cliff' was a small house at the end of a road that was next to the sea. From the house, a path led to a wall at the end of their garden. Through a gap in the wall, a set of steps went down to the sand.

The three brothers liked to sit on the steps in the sun and then listen to the call of the gulls. After all these years, the splash of the waves on the rocks was still a thrill for them. They sat there together every day and thought it was the best place on earth. They felt that there was no other place better than this.

2. Now can you draw the three brothers and a picture or a map to go with this story?

Common 'wh' words

The following words beginning with 'wh' can be useful to work on once the letter sound 'wh' has been introduced.

It is an ideal time to work on formulating questions, knowing the difference between a question and a statement and on using question marks.

Check which words are already known before you begin.

Use the word routines on pages 121–2 to study the words and to help the learners remember them.

what   **wh**en   **wh**ere   **wh**o   **wh**y   **wh**ich

'Wh' Question Symbols page 130

These picture symbols can be used as an aide-mémoire for learning the question words. Individual pupils can also use the sheet as a writing activity to practice formulating questions. They can make up questions for their friends or their teacher to answer.

Question Word Lotto and Pairs

The symbols on page 202 can also be copied and made into Lotto or a Pairs game where players have to formulate a question using the question word before they can place it on their base board or win a pair.

Question Match page 131

Can be used as a work sheet activity where a line is drawn from the question word to the rest of the question. It can also be cut up and laminated and used as a matching game.

See also the homework activities on page 136

Picture Symbols for Question Words

Can you make up a question using each word?
Remember to use a question mark.

What?	When?
Where?	Which?
Who?	Why?

Question Match

Can you read these 'wh' words? Match each one to the rest of a question.

What	did they run off?
Which	did he do?
Where	is the task?
Why	one is his?
What	quit his job?
Where	is the disk?
When	did he put it?
Who	can I fax you?
When	kicked him?
Why	will he be six?
Who	one is best?
Which	is he mad?

Homophones: Two, to and too

The homophones 'two', 'to' and 'too' can cause spelling difficulties for some learners. As with all homophones, concentrate on teaching the meaning of the words and their visual appearance. Use the word learning routines on pages 122 and 123. With most learners it is better to teach the three words separately to begin with.

Two

As the word 'two' is always a number word that represents two objects and is not used for anything else, teach this word first. It may be helpful to teach it alongside other number words and link it to 'twelve' and 'twenty' as they also begin with 'tw'. Learning the words 'two', 'twenty' and 'twelve' may also be linked to work on the letter sound 'tw' and linked to the picture clue 'twins' (page 62) as long as the pupil is not likely to be confused by the difference in pronunciation.

Learning the word 'two' can also be linked to work on plural 's' (page 98)

Too

The word 'too' means 'also' or 'as well as'. Teach the learner to see if these words can be used instead of the word 'too' in the sentence they want to write. If they can then it is 'too' that they need to use.

'Too' also means 'excessively' as in 'too much' or 'too hot'.

To

Although 'to' is the most common of the three homophones, it is quite difficult to explain. Teaching the meaning of the other two first sometimes results in this one falling into place. If it is not the number two or 'as well as' or 'too much' then use 'to' !

'To' is used as part of a verb or doing word as in 'to sit' or 'to chat' or it is used when someone is talking about 'going to' somewhere as in 'went to' or 'ran to'.

The 'Two', 'Too' and 'To' picture symbols on page 133 can be used as a prompt for writers to help them choose the correct spelling.

Sentence Dictation

Sentence dictation can be used once the three homophones have been taught to reinforce making the correct choice. The pupils can have the picture symbols on view if needed.

See also the homework activities on page 137

The 'Two', 'too' and 'to' Activity Sheet (page 134) can be used as an independent activity once the homophones have been learned. The symbols on page 133 can be used alongside this if needed.

Picture Symbols for Two, to and too

Which word do I need?

two	too

2 two

too hot

to	too

went to

me too

Sentences for Two, to and too

Can you fill in the right word?

1. I went _____ the shops.

2. I want to go _____.

3. Tim has _____ eggs for lunch.

4. It was _____ hot in the sun.

5. I am going _____ stop and rest.

6. Nick ran _____ catch the bus.

7. Gus sips his drink and Tim sips his _____.

8. Liz has _____ quid to spend.

9. Pam is going _____ the match.

Can you mark these sentences?

Tick the ones that are right. Change the ones that are wrong.

1. Tom is too quick for me.

2. Fran was ill and had to pills.

3. Rick swam back too the sand.

4. Trish is going to whisk the eggs.

5. Gran has glasses two.

6. Jack chats too Jill.

Literacy homework

Name

Return by

Words that begin with 'th': What to do

You will need a newspaper or magazine.

1. Try and find some of these words in the paper.

2. Draw a line under them.

the   this   then   they   there   that

3. Were there any words you didn't find?

4. Did you find any other words that begin with 'th' ?

5. Bring the newspaper to school.

This work had: Parent signature/comment

☐ no help

☐ some help

☐ a lot of help

Literacy homework

Name

Return by

Question words that begin with 'wh': What to do

1. Use each of these words to make up a question to ask a friend.

2. Write the questions down.

3. Who are you going to ask?

what when where who why which

This work had: **Parent signature/comment**

☐ no help

☐ some help

☐ a lot of help

Literacy homework

Name

Return by

Homophones 'two', 'to' and 'too': What to do

Homophones are words that sound the same but look different.

1. Draw a picture for each of these –
   '**two** cats'   '**too** cold'   '**to** run'

2. Now can you use '**two**' '**too**' and '**to**' and make three different pictures?

3. Write down what they are underneath

This work had: **Parent signature/comment**

☐ no help

☐ some help

☐ a lot of help

How Parents can Help

Literacy Homework

Dear Parents,

Each week your child will have some literacy homework to practise what has been covered in class. It also keeps you in touch with their learning. The type of homework given will depend on your child's needs.

The usual day for literacy homework is _____ and it is to be returned on_____.

The homework slip that is sent home tells you what work has to be done and when it is to be sent back. Talk about the work and help read any instructions. When the homework is finished ask your child to read it to you. Try to send homework back on time. It may be needed for a lesson in class.

It is alright to help your child if needed. Circle the slip at the bottom to say if you have given 'no help', 'some help' or 'a lot of help'. There is also space for you to add more comments if you wish. Please sign the bottom of the slip before sending it back.

If anything extra is needed for the homework it will say so at the top of the slip. For example, sometimes the work might be finding words in a newspaper, reading food packets or using the 'Yellow Pages'. If you haven't got something that is mentioned, please let me know. If writing paper is needed it will be sent home with the work, if not this means that your child can write on the homework slip. The back can also be used.

I hope you have found this information helpful. Please feel free to contact me at school if you wish to discuss anything further.

Best wishes,

Literacy homework

Name

Return by

_____ **: What to do**

This work had: **Parent signature/comment**

☐ no help

☐ some help

☐ a lot of help

Literacy homework

Name

Return by

_____ **: What to do**

This work had: **Parent signature/comment**

☐ no help

☐ some help

☐ a lot of help

The Alphabet

- A set of alphabet cards or magnetic letters on the fridge can be used to practise alphabetic order. Split the alphabet in to four sections to learn.

/abcd/   /efghijkl/   /mnopqr/   /stuvwxyz/

- Ask your child to look away while you take away a letter. Can they say which one is missing?

- For younger children match the letters to those in an alphabet book. Practise saying the names of the letters. Draw their shapes in the air or over the letters in the book with a finger.

- Talk about the pictures in the book. Look at the first letter of each word. Does your child know its name? Find it together in an alphabet set.

- For older children use a picture dictionary or the Yellow Pages in the same way.

- Make your own alphabet scrap book. The book needs a page for each letter. Stick in a picture of something beginning with each letter. Use magazine cuttings, drawings or computer clip art. The scrap book can have a theme, depending on your child's age and interest, such as animals, cars or pop stars.

- Look for other things in the home that have alphabetic order for example – telephone directories, address books, mobile phone address books, and indexes for books such as cookery books or car manuals.

Listening to Sounds

- When you are sharing books and talking with your child. Play a listening game together. Listen to the sounds that begin words. Do the words begin with the same sound or a different one?

- Play 'I spy with my little eye something that begins with the first sound in cat'.

- Make up names for family and friends that have the same sound at the beginning of each word, for example Marvellous Mum, Dazzling Dad! You can make up pretend football teams or pop stars names in the same way.

- Play 'The Hungry Hamster' game where you list all the things the hamster likes to eat that begin with the same sound, for example, 'The Hungry Hamster likes to eat biscuits, bananas, beans, etc.

- Play 'Kim's game'. Put six objects on a tray. Cover them with a cloth and take one away. Can your child say what is missing and the sound it begins with? The objects used will depend on your child's age, younger children might like to use toys, and older children might prefer objects from a pencil case or makeup bag.

- Say short poems and rhymes together. Which words sound the same at the end? They are the words that rhyme. Make up poems and jingles that have rhyming words – the sillier the better!

- Older children might like to listen to song lyrics in the same way. If you have access to the internet, many music sites have the words to songs on them.

How Print Works

- When you share a book with your child, point to the title of the book and talk about what it is called. Point to the name of the author and read the name. Have you read any more books together by the same person?

- Encourage your child to turn the pages and point to where you should read. Ask your child to point to the words as you read the them.

- The words 'first' and 'last' are very important for your child to understand when looking at the order of letters or words on a page. Put objects in a line and practise this, which one is first, which one is last? Say a list of three words. Which word did you say first? Which word was at the end? You can do the same with letters and sounds too.

- Help your child understand the difference between words and letters. When you are sharing a book, play a pointing game. Ask your child, "Can you point to a word?" "Can you point to a letter?" "Can you point to the first word on this page?" "Can you point to the last word in this sentence?" "Can you point to the first letter in this word?' "Can you point to the last letter?"

There are lots of other things to find out too.

- Can they say how many words are in a sentence you have read? How many letters are in a word that you point to?

- Are there any capital letters on a page? How many more can they find?

- Are there any full stops? How many full stops are on the page?

- Are there any question marks or speech marks to find?

- Older children can do the same with newspapers, magazines, computer print outs, e-mails and text messages.

Reading and Writing Together

- Try to spend a short time two or three times a week when you do some reading or writing together. A few short minutes spent in this way are better than one long session.

- Let your child see you reading, it helps to show that reading is important to you.

- Let your child see you writing. Involve them in writing notes, greeting cards, shopping lists, form filling, addressing envelopes, writing letters and e-mails.

- When you are writing, try not to use capital letters all the time. Capital letters are used at the beginning of a sentence and for the first letter of a name, unless you are filling in a form.

- Remember reading and writing doesn't always have to be with books, other things such as comics, magazines, 'teletext', e-mails, text messages, web pages, timetables, recipes, food packets and shopping lists, etc., are all good activities.

- Talk about what you have read together. It is important for your child to understand what he or she read. If it is a story, talk about what has happened so far and what might happen next? Was it a good story? Which was the best bit? If it was factual, was the information useful or interesting?

- When you are reading, if your child comes to a word he or she can't read wait a few seconds before you say what it is. Can your child guess the word from the pictures or the story? Does saying the first sound help? If not, then tell them the word and carry on reading.

- When your child is writing and needs help with spelling a word, encourage guessing first. Listen to the sounds in the word. Which sound comes first? Which one is at the end? Your child can write those parts of the word and you can fill in the rest. If you have a dictionary, use it to check the word afterwards to see if it was right.

- If there is a library near you then take your child along. Look for books that you can enjoy together. You can also borrow audio books, videos, CDs to listen to and go on the internet there too.

Making an Assessment

Making an assessment

Use this section to help decide on learning objectives and where to start teaching.

The Assessment Menu (page 152) helps decide which assessments are to be carried out and keeps track of the process. Your own records may replace some of the ones given here.

The Literacy Interview (pages 154–5) seeks to establish the learner's views of their literacy, their aspirations and interests. These can then be included in their learning programme.

Concepts About Print (page 156) is adapted from the work of Clay (1993) and finds out if the learner understands literacy terms and conventions and how books work. You will need a book at an appropriate level and of interest and two small pieces of card. Check that the book contains all the punctuation marks you will need.

Making A Running Record (page 150) This simple technique takes a little practice, but is well worth the effort as it supplies such valuable information on the learner's application of reading strategies to a whole text. Use the information on pages 150-151 to teach yourself how to carry this out. For those who wish to go into this further, Clay (1993) gives a more detailed account.

The Reading Strategies Assessment Sheet (page 157) is filled in after carrying out a running record.

Assessment of Writing is carried out through the learner completing the sheet on page 158 and the teacher recording observations made on page 159. It is always interesting to see the pupil's response when asked to create a list of words, some do this confidently and at length, others are at a loss where to begin and need some suggestions.

Alphabet and Dictionary Skills are assessed through page 162. You will also need a set of wooden or plastic letter shapes and a dictionary. Shaped letters are preferable to letters written on cards as this gives a chance to look at letter orientation.

Phonological Awareness Skills are assessed aurally through the sheet on page 160. See page 12 for further background reading in this area.

The Letter Sound Recognition Sheets on pages 163–4 require the learner to 'say the sound' represented by a letter and to generate two different words that begin with the target sound/s. Giving two words lessens the chance of the learner supplying their stock answer for such occasions. If a learner gives a word that begins with the target sound but is represented by a different letter then mark that as correct, for example, 'giraffe' for the sound 'j'. It is the ability to generate a word beginning with the same sound that is being

assessed. You can teach the vagaries of the English spelling system later. The words given by the learner also help to identify any confusion they might have between similar sounds such as g/k or d/t. In addition, if the learner is working visually rather than by sound they might say 'shoe' for a word beginning with 's'. Such errors should be recorded in the comments box.

The Spelling of Dictated Words on page 165 assesses whether letter sound knowledge is used. Many learners identify their sounds but make no use of these in their spelling.

Word Recognition of the NLS High Frequency Words can be recorded on page 166–7.

Further Assessment

A standardised assessment of reading accuracy, rate and comprehension with analysis of reading errors can be gained through the use of the **Neale Analysis of Reading Ability** (Nelson, 1997) or the **Individual Reading Analysis** (Vincent and de la Mare 1990).

Broomfield and Combley (2003) gives further information on assessment in action through case studies of individual learners.

Hatcher (2001) contains a detailed assessment of phonological awareness and a teaching programme.

The Single Word Spelling Test (Sacre and Masterson, 2000) is a diagnostic spelling assessment linked to the National Literacy Strategy with word lists for teaching.

Carrying out a Running Record

Choose an unfamiliar book at an appropriate level for the learner to read. It will need to produce a few errors, but should not be too difficult. Ask the learner to read aloud a section of approximately one hundred words (with beginners this may mean using more than one book). As the learner reads, the assessor records the reading on a blank sheet of paper in the following way.

Make a tick each time a word is read correctly. Record these in a line representing the words on the page; afterwards you will be able make a comparison with the real text. To help you keep track, start a new line of ticks each time a new line in the book occurs.

Record all errors made. Instead of a tick, write down exactly what was said or attempted, even if it was just an initial sound. The errors will be analysed afterwards to provide valuable teaching advice.

Words omitted are recorded with a dash.

Words refused and supplied by the teacher are recorded with a 'T'.

Words added are written in above an insertion mark and included in the error count.

Use 'SC' to record self corrections. These are words that were initially read incorrectly and then self corrected by the reader, without prompting from the assessor.

Further notes on use of picture clues, fluency, finger pointing, loss of place, expression, confidence and response to punctuation are also useful.

Check understanding. At the end of the running record ask the reader a few 'why' questions based on the text to see if the passage has been read with understanding.

Add up all the errors If the number of errors is above one in ten, then the text was at a level too difficult for the learner to read and understand independently

Analyse the Reading Errors Compare the running record with the text read and make notes on the 'Reading Strategies' sheet on page 157. Looking closely at the errors will give useful information on the techniques the learner was using, how successful they were in this and which ones they did not attempt. It will help you decide on their strengths and weaknesses and guide their learning programme. In order to do this, first classify the errors into the following categories, by asking yourself a set of questions. You will need to make an educated guess about the strategy you think the learner was most likely using (you can never be absolutely sure). This is why you need to look

Making an assessment

at a whole range of errors rather than one or two, in this way a trend emerges which is more reliable. Sometimes an error will demonstrate more than one type of reading behaviour, for example the use of an initial sound alongside context. Distinguishing between the use of visual and phonic clues is not always possible, to be sure of the latter you need to hear the reader attempting to 'sound out' the word.

Visual Does the word read look similar to the actual word in the text, i.e. does it have a similar length, shape and/or letters?

Phonic Did the reader try to use letter sounds? These attempts or lack of them can be compared alongside the letter sound assessment on page 163. Is the learner trying to make use of this knowledge when reading an unfamiliar text?

Grammatical Is the word read likely to occur in that position in an English sentence? Was it a good grammatical guess in line with the rest of the sentence?

Contextual Did the reader try to use knowledge of the world, the story or the pictures to guess a word? Did it make sense, even if it was wrong? Errors in this category give further information on comprehension alongside the 'why questions' you have asked.

Refusals Did the reader make any attempt at the word? If they merely look to the teacher for help each time, they show a lack of independence and confidence in their ability to use reading techniques.

Self Corrections Did these happen without prompting? If so, they are not counted as errors, as they suggest the reader is thinking about meaning and becoming independent.

An example of a simple running record and analysis is set out below.

Text The man jogged slowly along the road.
He stopped by the lamp post for a rest.

Running Record ✓ ✓ jogging slow ✓ ✓ street ✓ stop ✓ ✓ limp T ✓ ✓ ret.

'Jogging' and 'stop' are possible grammatical errors and work on suffix 'ed' may be helpful. 'Street' suggests that the learner is using context but is not using this alongside letter sound knowledge, a strategy combining the two should be encouraged. 'Limp' may be a visual error or a vowel discrimination problem, attempts at reading more words with the 'i' sound in them will help decide. Refusal of the word 'post' and 'ret' for rest suggest that work on end blends such as 'st' may be useful. There was no evidence of self correction.

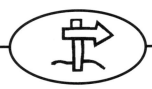

Assessment Menu

Name

Date

- Literacy Interview (page 154–5)
  1. Discussion about literacy.

- Reading skills (pages 156–7)
  1. Concepts about Print (page 156)
  2. Reading Strategies (page 157). Carry out a running record using a book at a suitable level. Note use of supporting skills, visual, phonic, context and reading behaviours such as fluency, tracking, confidence, self correction and self-help skills.

- Writing skills (pages 158–9)
  1. Writing own full name and address
  2. Writing the alphabet in sequence
  3. Generating own list of words that they are confident in writing independently
  4. Writing a few sentences about self
  Note handedness, grip, position, formation, size, reversals, and joins, use of capitals and punctuation, spacing, organisation on the page.

- Alphabet and dictionary skills (page 162)
  1. Knowledge of alphabet names (test these out of sequence)
  2. Alphabetic order – using wooden/plastic letters
  3. Writing individual letters (out of sequence) to dictation
  4. Using the dictionary – first letter (all assessments), second letter (optional)

- Phonological Awareness (pages 160–1)
  1. Rhyme – can they say if word pairs rhyme or not?
  2. Alliteration – can they tell if word pairs begin with the same sound or not?
  3. Syllable blending – can blend 2/3/4/syllables into words?
  4. Syllable segmentation – can they segment words into 2/3/4 syllables?
  5. Phoneme blending – can they blend 2/3/4/5 phonemes into words?
  6. Phoneme segmentation – can they segment words into 2/3/4/5 phonemes?

- Letter Sound Links (pages 163–5)
  1. Naming initial sounds and generation of two words for each sound.
  2. Writing dictated cvc words.
  3. Writing dictated ccvc, cvcc and ccvcc words.

- Word recognition (pages 166–7)
  1. National Literacy Strategy High Frequency words set 1
  2. National Literacy Strategy High Frequency words set 2

- Standardised Tests
  1. Check records, note results, date, if any further testing needed.

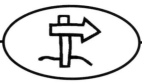

Assessment Summary

Name		Class	DOB	Date
Background information *(also see Literacy Interview)*				
Spoken language				
Concepts about print				
Phonological awareness	Alliteration		Rhyme	
	Syllable		Phoneme	
Alphabet and dictionary skills				
Letter–sound Links				
Word recognition	HF1		HF2	
Reading strategies				
Standardised test results				
Handwriting				
Spelling	cvc	ccvc	cvcc	ccvcc
Free writing (assessment sample attached)				

Literacy Interview

Name

Date

Literacy Support is here to give extra help with reading and writing. We want to find out how we can help you.

1. Let's talk about you first.

   • How old are you?

   • Where do you live?

   • Who lives with you?

   • Have you any pets?

   • Have you any hobbies?

   • What do you like to do best at school?

2. Now let's talk about reading. Is it something you find easy or difficult?

3. Do you like reading?

4. What do you like to read?

5. Do you read at home?

6. Do you ever visit a library?

7. What do you find difficult about reading?

8. What do you do when you come to a word that you can't read?

9. Now let's talk about writing. Is handwriting something you find easy or difficult?

10. Do you like handwriting?

11. What do you find difficult about handwriting?

12. When you are asked to write a story or some news, do you find it easy to write everything you want to say?

13. Do you like writing?

14. Do you ever write at home? What do you write?

15. What do you find difficult about writing?

16. Do you find spelling words easy or difficult?

17. What do you find difficult about spelling?

18. When you want to spell a word that you don't know, what do you do?

19. Would you like extra help with your reading and writing?

20. Would you do homework?

21. Would someone help you at home?

22. Does anyone else in your family have difficulty with reading and writing?

23. We have talked a lot about things that you find difficult. Now tell me something that you are good at!

24. Is there anything else you want to tell me?

Check files for the following and note here any information regarding:

Stage of Code of Practice/Level of Additional Support
Eyesight
Hearing
Speech and language
Physical/co-ordination
Relevant medical issues
Relevant information from Educational Psychology
Other

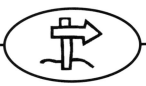

Concepts About Print

| Name | | Date | |

1	*Hand the pupil a book with the spine forwards.* 'Show me the front/back of this book.'	
2	'Can you point to the title/name of the book?'	
3	'Can you point to the author's name (or name of person who wrote the book?)'	
4	'Now open the book and point to where we start reading.'	
5	'Show me with your finger which way we go when we read. Where do we go when we get to the end of the line?'	
6	'Can you point to each word of this sentence as I read it?'	
7	*Teacher opens the book at a double page spread.* 'Which page do we read first?'	
8	*Teacher puts two small pieces of card either end of a sentence.* 'Can you close the cards up until only one word is showing? Now show me two words.'	
9	*Teacher puts two small pieces of card either end of a sentence.* 'Can you close the cards up until only one letter is showing? Now show me two letters.'	
10	'Can you put your finger at the beginning of a sentence? Put another finger where that sentence ends.'	
11	*Teacher points to a letter.* 'What is the name of this letter? And this one?'	
12	*Teacher points to another letter.* 'What sound does this letter represent? And this one?'	
13	'Point to the first word in this sentence. Point to the last word.'	
14	'Point to the first letter in this word. Point to the last letter.'	
15	'Can you find a capital letter on this page? When do we use a capital letter?'	
16	'Can you find a full stop on this page? When do we use a full stop?'	
17	'Can you find a question mark on this page? When do we use a question mark?'	
18	'Can you find any speech marks on this page? When do we use speech marks?'	
19	'Can you find an exclamation mark? When do we use an exclamation mark?'	

Reading Strategies

| Name | Date | Title |

1. Carry out a running record using an **unfamiliar** book at an appropriate level (see pages 150–1).

2. Note reading strategies observed (both successful/ unsuccessful):

- Visual

- Phonic

- Grammatical

- Context

- Fluency and speed

- Tracking, use of finger, loss of place, etc.

- Confidence

- Self-correction

- Self-help/ reliance on teacher

- Comprehension

- Other

Writing – Pupil Sheet

Write your name _____ Today's Date _____

Your Address_____

_____

_____

_____

Write the alphabet_____

_____

_____

Write some words you can spell for yourself.

_____   _____

_____   _____

_____   _____

_____   _____

Write a few sentences about yourself.

_____

_____

_____

_____

_____

Writing Observations

Name

Date

Note relevant comments regarding:

- Right / Left Handed

- Paper position

- Body position

- Formation

- Reversals

- Joins

- Appropriate use of capitals   Yes   No

- Appropriate use of full stops   Yes   No

- Spacing

- Organisation on page

- Other

Phonological Awareness 1

Name   Date

Only the assessor should be able to see the words.

Alliteration:

Do these words begin with the same sound?

Practice :

Box   Hat

Biscuit   Balloon

Test:

1. doll   door
2. see   sit
3. house   feet
4. leg   leaf
5. table   candle
6. picnic   pillow
7. window   dentist
8. glove   glass

Score:

Tell me a word that begins with the same sound as...

1. mouse
2. cup
3. salt
4. table
5. ball
6. girl
7. fog
8. shell

Score:

Rhyme:

Do these words rhyme?

Practice:

Pin   tin

Hat   zip

Test

1. hot   cap
2. sing   ring
3. lock   rock
4. mouse leg
5. four   pour
6. ladder   swimming
7. castle   basket
8. tea   flea

Score:

Tell me a word that rhymes with ....

1. tin
2. cat
3. van
4. sock
5. peg
6. den
7. pear
8. key

Score:

Phonological Awareness 2

Name

Date

Syllable blending:

What word am I saying? (Leave one second interval between each syllable)
1. ta-ble
2. pen-cil
3. well-ing-ton
4. in-ter-net
5. de-co-ra-tion
6. ma-ca-ro-ni

Score:

Syllable segmentation:

Can you break these words into syllables?
1. carpet   (car-pet)
2. sandwich   (sand-wich)
3. radio   (ra-di-o)
4. elephant   (el-e-phant)
5. experiment   (ex-pe-ri-ment)
6. technology   (tech-nol-o-gy)

Score

Phoneme blending

What word am I saying? (Leave one second between each phoneme)
1. t-o͞o
2. c-a-n
3. p-ai-n
4. ch-i-ll
5. m-i-n-t
6. l-i-s-t
7. s-t-i-l-t

Score:

Phoneme segmentation

Can you break these words into sounds?
1. go (g-oh)
2. shoe (sh-oo)
3. pat (p-a-t)
4. list (l-i-s-t)
5. camp (c-a-m-p)
6. crate (c-r-ay-t)
7. slant (s-l-a-n-t)

Score:

Alphabet and Dictionary Skills

Name	Date

1. **Naming letters of the alphabet out of sequence**

m b n v c x l z k p j o h
u i g y f t d r s e a w q

2. **Ordering a full set of wooden or plastic letters into alphabetic order** (Teacher records the exact sequence and orientation below)

3. **Writing individual letters to dictation** (pupil should not be able to see these letters)

f r s t p k c b h q m z w
a x e d v g y n j u i l o

4. **Use of dictionary** – What is a dictionary for? (spelling and meaning)

5. **Use of dictionary – First letter** After finding each word listed below, ask 'Which way will you turn next?' Note scanning skills when searching for the word. Pupils should not be able to see the target words.

   house   man   dog   school

6. **Use of dictionary – second letter** (optional) – 'Can you explain how you know where to look for each word?' Pupils should not be able to see the target words.

   cat   tree   sit   fly

Single Letter Sounds

Name

Date

Sound (What sound does this letter represent?)	Word (Tell me a word that begins with that sound)	Word (Tell me another word that begins with that sound)	Observations/Comments
i			
t			
p			
n			
s			
a			
d			
h			
e			
c			
b			
k			
r			
m			
y			
l			
f			
o			
g			
u			
j			
v			
w			
x			
z			
q			
Total Score			

Initial Consonant Blends and Digraphs

Name

Date

Sound (What sound does this letter represent?)	Word (Tell me a word that begins with that sound)	Word (Tell me another word that begins with that sound)	Observations/Comments
t h			
s h			
c h			
wh			
s t			
s p			
s n			
s k			
s m			
s w			
d r			
p r			
t r			
b r			
fr			
g r			
cr			
s l			
fl			
bl			
g l			
c l			
p l			
t w			
Total Score			

Letter Sounds – Spelling Dictated Words

Each word should be dictated clearly with no exaggerations. If a learner has difficulty with section one, then the later sections need not be assessed at this point.

Section One – Consonant Vowel Consonant (CVC)

1. wig	8. kit
2. Dan	9. led
3. top	10. run
4. vet	11. bus
5. cod	12. fox
6. hot	13. yam
7. jab	14. zip

Section Two – Consonant blend/digraph, Vowel, Consonant (CCVC)

1. brag	8. thin
2. chip	9. blot
3. flan	10. cram
4. grin	11. drug
5. plum	12. Fred
6. whip	13. glut
7. trot	14. shed

Section Three – Consonant, Vowel, Consonant Blend/Digraph (cvcc)

1. Beth	8. hand
2. colt	9. kept
3. dent	10. silk
4. gasp	11. desk
5. much	12. ramp
6. rock	13. gulp
7. lost	14. rash

Section Four – Consonant Blend/Digraph, Vowel, Consonant Blend/Digraph (CCVCC)

1. trash	8. scans
2. blank	9. thump
3. crisp	10. chest
4. drips	11. bring
5. froth	12. shelf
6. grant	13. swift
7. plush	14. trend

Word Recognition HFW1

Name	Date

I	to
it	on
in	no
is	look
a	for
at	go
and	going
said	dog
dad	big
he	get
see	you
can	up
cat	mum
are	we
me	went
am	was
my	away
yes	the
day	this
like	they
play	she
all	
of	**Total:**

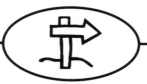

Word Recognition HFW2

Name

Date

as	name	off	your	water
an	time	old	house	way
did	by	once	laugh	were
his	many	one	must	would
has	may	or	our	who
had	ball	people	pull	will
seen	call	school	cut	next
can't	called	so	just	than
take	help	some	jump	that
bed	last	too	have	then
be	little	took	over	these
back	if	again	very	there
been	after	dig	love	their
her	first	girl	loved	three
here	half	good	live	them
ran	boy	got	lived	another
sister	do	night	down	push
tree	don't	about	how	should
came	door	because	new	much
him	from	but	now	with
made	home	could	saw	what
make	more	out	two	when
man	not	us	want	where

Planning a Learning Programme

A learning programme is built from the areas of need identified through assessment. Key headings are used to set learning objectives for each learner or group of learners using the sheet on page 171. Some will need a carefully balanced programme using all of the areas; others will need to work on a smaller set of priorities.

Learning objectives form the broad basis from which short-term planning and more specific targets such as those needed for IEPs can be developed. For example, the learning objective *'to recognise and use consonant blends'* might have a more detailed IEP target of *'to read and spell ccvc and cvcc words which contain 's' blends.'* An individual lesson related to this might involve learning to use the blend 'st' at the beginning and end of words.

Teaching and Learning Activities for each aspect of a learner's programme can be drawn from the relevant section of this resource pack. Use the handbook for *Overcoming Dyslexia* for further ideas.

The short-term planner on page 173, is linked to the learning objectives sheet. It offers a way

of organising lessons to ensure they are carefully structured and cover the range of literacy learning activities each learner or group needs. It also provides a method of recording learning outcomes which inform future teaching.

Although the planner is divided into seven different literacy activities, it is not expected that each lesson should contain every one of these. Over a series of lessons it will become obvious when the content needs to be broadened into other areas and new learning in one area can be applied within another.

The planner should not be used in a linear way. The order in which the activities within a lesson are carried out will vary and can be indicated on the plan through numbering the sections. See the example plan on page 172.

During a lesson, tick the sections that have been learned without any difficulty and make brief notes against anything that caused a problem or needs further practice. A further note under the section 'Next Lesson' will give a head start to future planning.

Integrated Reading and Writing

Within the planner, the terms 'integrated reading' and 'integrated writing' refer to activities that integrate the separate literacy skills that have been learned into a wider context. For example, having taught a particular letter sound, the teacher should plan for opportunities that encourage the learner to put this skill into practice when reading a text or writing a story (see page 68).

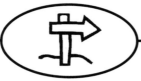

Learning Objectives

Name		Class	DOB	Date
Literacy Skill	Objectives			
Concepts About Print				
Alphabet and Dictionary				
Phonological Awareness				
Letter Sound Links				
Word Recognition				
Integrated Reading				
Integrated Writing				

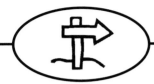

Example Lesson Planner

Name		Class		Date

Literacy Skill	Plan	Outcome
Concepts About Print		
Alphabet and Dictionary	6. Find 'look' ✔ ' like' ✔ 'little' ✘ in dictionary	
Phonological Awareness	3. Listen for 'l' at the beginning/end of words lip, little, last, call, sail, smell, list, pool, laugh, Lisa ✔	Good listening
Letter/sound Links	1. Introduce new sound 'l' ✔ 2. Make memory card ✔ 4. Build words level one – lip, lad, lick, Len, lid ✔ 5. level two- slip, plan, black, slid ✔	Needed help with 'sl' – built 'sid' and 'sip' missing out 'l' in 'slip' and 'slid'
Word Recognition	7. Learn HFW 'like' ✔	
Integrated Reading		
Integrated Writing	8. Dictated sentence 'Cats like milk.' (level 2) ✔ Own ideas for sentence/s with teacher support using 'I like'	Wrote 'I like football.' and 'I like ipswich.' – no help needed for 'football' No capital I.
Homework	9. Find telephone numbers in 'Yellow Pages' for a leisure centre, a locksmith, a library and a laundrette	
Next lesson	Begin work on 'l' blends starting with 'sl.' Reminder about capitals for names of places and people.	

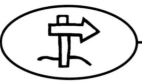

Lesson Planner

Name	Class		Date

Literacy Skill	Plan	Outcomes
Concepts About Print		
Alphabet and Dictionary		
Phonological Awareness		
Letter/sound Links		
Word Recognition		
Integrated Reading		
Integrated Writing		
Homework		
Next lesson		

References

Broomfield H, Combley M (2003) Overcoming Dyslexia: A Practical Handbook for the Classroom. London: Whurr Publishers.

Bryant P, Bradley L (1985) Children's Reading Problems. Oxford: Basil Blackwell.

Clay M (1993) An Observation Survey of Early Literacy Achievement. Auckland: Heinemann.

Hatcher PJ (2001) Sound Linkage: An Integrated Programme for Overcoming Reading Difficulties, 2nd Edition. London: Whurr Publishers.

Hickey K (1977) Dyslexia: A Language Training Course for Teachers and Learners (3rd edn 2001, Combley M ed. 2001) London: Whurr.

Nelson MD (1997) Neale Analysis of Reading Ability (British Adaptation by Christophers U, Whetton C). Windsor: NFER-Nelson.

Sacre L, Masterson J (2000) Single Word Spelling Test. Windsor: NFER-Nelson.

Vincent D, de la Mare M (1990) Individual Reading Analysis. Windsor: NFER-Nelson.

Useful Resources

Broomfield H, Combley M (2003) Overcoming Dyslexia: A Practical Handbook for the Classroom. London: Whurr Publishers.

Clicker. Crick Computing, 123 The Drive, Northampton NN1 4SW, UK.

Hatcher PJ (2001) Sound Linkage: An Integrated Programme for Overcoming Reading Difficulties, 2nd Edition. London: Whurr Publishers.

Hickey K (1977) Dyslexia: A Language Training Course for Teachers and Learners (3rd edn 2001, Combley M ed. 2001) London: Whurr.

Mayer-Johnson Picture Symbols (1984) Mayer-Johnson Company PO Box 1579, Solana Beach, CA 92075-7579, USA.

Writing with Symbols. Widgit Software, 102 Radford Road, Leamington Spa, UK.

Index

Index

Index